Praise for *17 Rules Successful Companies Use to Attract and Keep Top Talent*

"This book is packed with lessons for every manager who aspires to attract and motivate talented people and build a great organization. Russo is able to ground the best conceptual ideas in the wisdom of his own deep experience and share it all in an easy-going conversational style."

—**M. Diane Burton**, Associate Professor of Management, Massachusetts Institute of Technology

"David Russo has spent a lifetime observing employees and organizations. His down-to-earth admonitions may at first blush seem obvious; however, they are pearls of wisdom. Leaders of big and small organizations would do well to heed his counsel and treat their people as if they were volunteers—as if every employee can indeed make a difference."

—**Thomas J. DeLong**, Harvard Business School, Philip J. Stomberg Professor of Management Practice and co-author of *When Professionals Have to Lead: A New Model for High Performance* (Harvard Business School Press, 2007)

"Passionate and dedicated workplaces of talented employees are within every leader's reach. David's been there. He knows. And he gives it to you straight. Apply his trademark, candid advice that you'll find in this book, and you will start seeing significant positive, profitable shifts in your company culture almost immediately. So listen up!"

—**Martha I. Finney**, President and CEO, Engagement Journeys, LLC and author of *The Truth About Getting the Best From People*

"David Russo is a thoughtful and reflective practitioner. His book, *17 Rules Successful Companies Use to Attract and Keep Top Talent*, should be read by top-level executives, as well as human resources managers, if they want to know what actually works with respect to the attraction and retention of talent. The practical example Russo provides, which comes from his knowledge and experience, makes this an extremely useful publication."

—**Fred K. Foulkes**, Professor of Organizational Behavior, Director, Human Resources Policy Institute, Boston University, School of Management

"This book is interesting, provocative, and deeply true. Russo's advice points the way for leaders to build and sustain high performance organizations. Beautifully free of jargon and silver bullets, Russo wisely focuses on common sense and consistent execution."

—**Cade Massey**, Professor of Organizational Behavior, Yale University, School of Management

"Russo packages a career of experience and insight into a set of rules that will save managers much heartache and a constant 'comfort' guide as they face a new people issue for the first time."

—**Dallas Salisbury**, President & CEO, Employee Benefit Research Institute

17 Rules Successful Companies Use to Attract and Keep Top Talent

17 Rules Successful Companies Use to Attract and Keep Top Talent

Why Engaged Employees Are Your
Greatest Sustainable Advantage

David Russo

Vice President, Publisher: Tim Moore
Associate Publisher and Director of Marketing: Amy Neidlinger
Acquisitions Editor: Jennifer Simon
Editorial Assistant: Pamela Boland
Development Editor: Russ Hall
Operations Manager: Gina Kanouse
Senior Marketing Manager: Julie Phifer
Publicity Manager: Laura Czaja
Assistant Marketing Manager: Megan Colvin
Cover Designer: Chuti Prasertsith
Managing Editor: Kristy Hart
Project Editor: Chelsey Marti
Copy Editor: Geneil Breeze
Proofreader: Leslie Joseph
Indexer: Erika Millen
Compositor: Jake McFarland
Manufacturing Buyer: Dan Uhrig

FT Press offers excellent discounts on this book when ordered in quantity for bulk purchases or special sales. For more information, please contact U.S. Corporate and Government Sales, 1-800-382-3419, corpsales@pearsontechgroup.com. For sales outside the U.S., please contact International Sales at international@pearson.com.

Company and product names mentioned herein are the trademarks or registered trademarks of their respective owners.

Printed in the United States of America

First Printing January 2010

ISBN-10: 0-13-714670-1
ISBN-13: 978-0-13-714670-3

Pearson Education LTD.
Pearson Education Australia PTY, Limited.
Pearson Education Singapore, Pte. Ltd.
Pearson Education North Asia, Ltd.
Pearson Education Canada, Ltd.
Pearson Educación de Mexico, S.A. de C.V.
Pearson Education—Japan
Pearson Education Malaysia, Pte. Ltd.

Library of Congress Cataloging-in-Publication Data

Russo, David F.
  17 rules successful companies use to attract and keep top talent : why engaged employees are your greatest sustainable advantage / David F. Russo.
    p. cm.
  ISBN-13: 978-0-13-714670-3 (hardback : alk. paper)
  ISBN-10: 0-13-714670-1 (hardback : alk. paper) 1. Personnel management. 2. Supervision of employees. 3. Leadership. 4. Industrial relations. I. Title. II. Title: Seventeen rules successful companies use to attract and keep top talent.
  HF5549 R789 2009

Alongside every fledging author there must be a special person who convinces him that he is much smarter than he knows he really is. Thanks Marsha!

Few people you met along the way will remember how smart you were, how much you accomplished, or even what you looked like, but everybody will remember how you made them feel.
—Harry Dawley

Contents

Foreword: Great Teams, Great People, Great Leaders

I first met David Russo at a Jimmy V. charity golf event, in North Carolina. Jim Valvano, the charismatic basketball coach of North Carolina State, died of cancer 12 years ago, and the V Foundation, which he founded before his death, raises funds for cancer research. So, it wasn't hard to pick out like-minded people at the charity event: Everyone was there to help raise money for a worthy cause and in memory of a great man. However, when I first met David, I immediately knew we would grow to be friends, and I sensed it after just a few minutes of chatting and a couple holes of golf. Why? Well, I recognized that he was one of my tribe. We have roots in Pittsburgh. His roots come from birth, and mine from a career that grew into a love affair with the town and its people—beautiful, honest, rough-and-tumble Pittsburgh. Plus, it turned out that we both shared a Catholic heritage. Moreover, David is a lifelong Pittsburgh Steelers fan, and as you might expect, I am kind of partial to that organization, having played there for 11 years, before and after I went to Vietnam.

As I got to know David over the years, I found we also share something else, and that is a clear understanding of what motivates people, what makes teams gel, and how to sustain that motivation and team spirit over a long period of time. The common understanding we share is that standout organizations—whether they are great professional sports teams (like our Steelers!) or great business organizations of almost any size—cannot be manufactured or concocted. A still-wet-behind-the-ears NFL general manager or a freshly minted MBA may think that greatness is formulaic, and that dream teams can be assembled, like parts from a kit, by buying talent and tossing it on the field. They may naively expect to win a Super Bowl, or capture a dominant market share as a matter of course. You can no more expect that level of instant performance from a team—even one comprised of great players—than you can expect that from a business organization that has paid top dollar for talent, yet lacks the mission, the vision, and the goals articulated by great leadership. To put it another way, you can no more conjure up or demand greatness from a team or a business than you can train basset hounds to drive a minivan. From my experience with the Steelers, David's experience at SAS, *and* the work we have both subsequently done as organizational and motivational consultants, one thing is abundantly clear: Great organizations are crafted with patience, great care, and honesty. They emerge only when great leadership articulates an honest and clear-eyed vision of a meaningful and successful future. If you think I'm being too idealistic, let me add that greatness is also about old-fashioned "play through the pain" hard work, overcoming obstacles, and making team members aware that they are part of something with potential for greatness. Equally important, all players—on the field or at the office—must know the role they play and understand exactly how they can contribute to outstanding results.

We can push this comparison even further, and the similarities hold true. Just as with an NFL team, where roles must be clear, so too must roles be clear in business. You can't have a general manager who thinks he's the coach, or the coach who thinks he's an owner. Yet at the same time, it has to be clear to each member of the organization what his role is and—something that David really drives home in this book—what part the *individual performance* contributes to team performance and overall desired direction. It is crucial that every player knows this on and off the field, whether it's a special teams player who is only out on the field three downs in a game, the defensive back who must defend both run and pass, or the assembly line worker whose quality assurance tests of product are the last line of defense against the tarnishing of a company's brand. When people see the role they play—as we did as Steelers players with the likes of Jack Lambert, Mean Joe Greene, L. C. Greenwood, Terry Bradshaw, Franco Harris, and myself—you start to recognize that people are proud to be part of the team, of contributing to something greater than themselves. You find that they contribute what David calls that "illusive discretionary effort" every single day, every single play...and not just at crunch time. That's what great leadership can bring forth in players in any organizational setting.

That said, I have come to discover in David and his writing, a kindred spirit that understands how people should be valued, encouraged, and inspired. And that's what this book is about and why I agreed to write this foreword. So, in that vein, let me talk for a moment about great teams and great companies. You see, in the business world, because of well-executed plays, great runs, and record returns, one company might put up great numbers in a single year, and maybe even win the "Super Bowl" of their business sector—an effort that leaves them at the top of the heap temporarily. But what I've focused my energy on, and what this book focuses, is not the company or the team that wins a "Super Bowl" now and then, but the team or the company that establishes *and sustains* dynasties.

Look at the NFL clubs that have done this, the NFL clubs that have had dominant runs: The Cowboys, the Forty Niners. The Packers of the 1960s. The Steelers of the 1970s, when we won four Super Bowls in six years. Believe me, those great runs, those years of sustained top performance, were no accident. The owners and general managers of those now-famous clubs didn't just toss a bunch of talent onto a playing field and hope for the best. These so-called dynasties were part of deliberate strategies, consistent leadership, and entrenched belief systems. All the great leaders of the past—Vince Lombardi, Bill Walsh, Chuck Noll—all these men were special in this way: They looked at their talent, indentified and acquired players to fill in the missing links, and then they created a vision for what these players were capable of becoming. They motivated them to achieve that, being careful to point out the importance of each role the individual players assumed. I realize that some of these great coaches had the advantage of team consistency before the dawn of free agency. But the modern dynasties do not have that advantage. Indeed, the players and the coaches both recognize that today, more than ever, players are "volunteers"—just as David Russo rightly points out that *employees* are volunteers in the workplace. In either setting, the clear articulation of vision and goals is sometimes *the only thing* that holds the talent together and crafts a team, and recognizing that is now doubly important in the NFL and in the business world.

This book provides a road map to achieve what I have lived in the NFL and what I have preached in my speaking career after the NFL. It sets down the rules. But as you get to know David over the course of this book, you'll realize these rules were not dreamed up by somebody high in a Skybox who hasn't been grinding it out on the field of play. David's been in the trenches, and he's worked with companies of all sizes, from start-ups, to the largest software companies in the world. So, in essence, I am here to vouch for his approach. I've seen it work magic, and I've seen it achieve greatness, a success that anyone is capable of, if they learn to become great leaders, and attend to the rules that follow in these great chapters.

—Rocky Bleier
   Renowned motivational speaker and former NFL star

Acknowledgments

This book could not have been produced without the help of many professional acquaintances, friends, and family, who either stimulated the thinking that produced the Rules or encouraged me to lend my voice to the discussion of high-performing companies and what it takes to craft them. Special thanks go to John Wagner of J. Wagner Media; Jeffrey Pfeffer of The Stanford University Business School; Jim Goodnight of SAS; Milton Moskowitz, Robert Levering, and Amy Lyman of the Great Place to Work Institute; and Harry F. Dawley of The Liggett Group (retired), who, knowingly or not, mentored, prodded, challenged, and/or encouraged me to write.

About the Author

David Russo is Principal and CEO of Eno River Associates, Inc., a consulting practice that helps executives build high-performing organizations by developing win-win relationships with the workforce. Mr. Russo has consulted with many global companies and organizations, including American Express, Johnson & Johnson, Minitab, Inc., American Eagle Outfitters, and the CIA. Before his retirement in 1999, he was the senior human resources executive for SAS Institute, the world's largest privately held software company, known as a perennial *Fortune* "Best Place to Work" for its quality work environment and focus on its people.

Introduction

I believe that I may know one of the first thoughts that came to your mind when you glanced at the title of this book: Where's this guy been for the last 18 months? *I don't have to worry about getting and retaining top talent because A) I really don't need more staff right now, and the streets are awash in talent; they're all begging for work! and B) even the talented and productive people I have are so happy just to be employed, they will tough out everything short of a Banana Republic Dictatorship to keep their jobs.*

Well, that certainly is one appraisal of today's employment market.

But it's "received wisdom."

And like most received wisdom, it's *dead wrong.*

In most cases, today's most capable and talented people are *not* unemployed. Indeed, they are the ones who've *held* their jobs in the downturn. Moreover, they are the ones that all companies are depending on, and whom great companies have gone to great lengths to retain. And an aggressive retention strategy, when followed in good times *and* bad, is a historical pattern that great companies follow, particularly in tough economic times, to great effect. Indeed, great companies don't just wait out downturns, they take advantage of them to position themselves for the inevitable recovery. (*Inevitable?* Yes, as Warren Buffet recently said, and I'd be a fool to disagree: "It is hard to 'short' the U.S. in the long term.")

Now, don't get me wrong. I am not a Pollyanna. Certainly, great companies husband their resources in slow times. They flex in size to respond to market conditions. They do pare the size of their workforces to meet economic realities and make other moves to reduce costs and control expenses. But they take advantage of slow and difficult times to shrewdly, prudently optimize processes and procedures, and *secure the services of the best people*, so they are ready to leap forward at the first sign of opportunity. There is continuing and overwhelming evidence that great companies are undertaking these preemptive actions today. Why? Well, for starters, it's a strategy that has proved very successful over the last 200 years or more. Moreover, attracting and retaining top talent is a *de rigueur* part of any route to survival, and its benefits are two-fold. First, obviously, you keep your key people (and retain all the resources you have put into training them and their institutional knowledge). But you also deprive your adversaries of the human resources that they can use to arm themselves against you.

Are you really prepared to gamble on a strategy that funnels your top people toward the exits and into the job market, knowing there's a high probability your competitor will pick them up, give them a laptop and an Internet connection and say, "You have but one job, my son. Use your unique knowledge to crush your previous employer." Believe me, there are many rusted, burnout hulks of companies along the road that didn't believe in the "people" part of the success equation, made that gamble...and lost.

In another respect, the recession has likely done a big favor to great companies. It has thinned the herd of competitors whose vitality was based on the crest of the wave of a powerful economy's demand for goods and services, and their availability in that seller's market. That culling process was hard to do during the "boom," because there was so much business to absorb. We have all heard over and over that in good times the simple fact of a company's *availability* counted as much as their *ability* when companies shopped for vendors. You also know as well as I what these "also-ran" companies" look like and how they operate: They pay no attention to sound business fundamentals—whether it was debt, cash reserves, cost controls, the quality and appropriateness of hires or employee retention—as they work to achieve a "sugar high" that makes a couple founders and maybe some top sales guys briefly rich. Well, the current recession has created an *acid test for them*, and it has threatened their ability to survive. In many cases, it has already flushed the weak and poorly run companies out of the market...and out of your hair. (Survivors don't question the hard-heartedness of evolution; they breathe a deep sigh of relief and resignedly say, *Well, survival of the fittest is a constant, and who's to argue with the course of nature!?*) Given the market conditions that have set the newest paradigm in motion, companies that survive the recession can emerge with an overwhelming competitive advantage, *if* they paid attention to business fundamentals, which invariably include attracting and retaining, with appropriate investment, the right people.

If you are looking for evidence of this, consider the value, stock prices, and sustainability of companies that have shown a commitment to the people in the workforce through prescribed leadership and management behavior. Apple, Merck, Rubbermaid, SAS, and Southwest Airlines are shining examples of companies that survive tough times and come out the other end of the storms as dominant players with astounding competitive advantage.

Do you honestly think that these companies and others like them treated their top talent with disdain over the last two years? Or assumed that all the best people would stay simply because the job market tanked? Or behaved as though the economic catastrophe we have known over the last two years would last forever? If so, you have a fatal misperception of how companies work and what makes them valuable over time.

Indeed, these companies have recognized that there is *always* a market for talent. And just like a good real estate magnate who retains his legacy holdings during a recession, as he snaps up property to emerge *twice* as big and *twice* as strong after a downturn, these companies—when rich in foresight—snap up and secure talent to prepare to dominate.

The only remaining question is this: Will you dominate...or will you be the victim of companies far better prepared than you who misperceived the recession as a general buyers' market for talent?

Your choice.

But let me tell you something, you better not have it wrong, fatally wrong.

There is old business adage and quotation, originated by Dale Carnegie, we all know: "When fate gives you a lemon, make lemonade". Now I know some of you reading are saying, *This Russo fellow is in an ivory tower somewhere, and I'm battling it out in the streets where different rules apply. I didn't just get a lemon or two in this recession...I got lemons, delivered free, by the metric ton!*

Fact is, I am not in an ivory tower; I'm a businessman who has firsthand experience with the behaviors of some truly great companies, and who—sticking to the principles in this book—has advised others on the benefits of proactive retention strategies. So I do understand the urge to panic. In fact, I embrace it.

Embrace panic?

Yes, and I do so with this quote from Thomas Paine's *The Crisis* in mind: "*Panics, in some cases, have their uses; they produce as much good as hurt. Their duration is always short; the mind soon grows through them and acquires a firmer habit than before. But their peculiar advantage is, that they are the touchstones of sincerity and hypocrisy, and bring things and men to light, which might have lain forever undiscovered.*"

In an economic sense, without the presence of "panic," it is less likely that the unworthy businesses are exposed, and the great companies are able to distinguish and separate themselves.

Now that's lemonade!

So, how does this attracting and retention strategy work in the "real world," in which organizations struggle to remain viable and significant in spite of problems, circumstantial or self-inflicted?

The writer of the Preface to this book is Robert "Rocky" Bleier. Rocky is a former, renowned National Football League running back for the Pittsburgh Steelers and the winner of four Super Bowl rings. What makes his willingness to do the introduction so special to me is not the fame that came with his football successes, his heroic effort in the service of his country, or that I can call him a friend. Instead, it's the relationship of Rocky's personal story, which is told in his own book, *Fighting Back*, to the story of a business that survived years of difficulty, lack of success, and subpar performance and evolved into an envied sports and entertainment franchise.

In the 38 seasons from 1933 through 1971, the Pittsburgh Steelers of the National Football League built an awful record of only 172 wins, 271 losses, and 18 ties. In all that time they had only 8 winning seasons and had *never* played for a championship, coming close only once—in 1936. Talk about a business that was deep in recession! But wait. In the 37 seasons since 1971, the Steelers have appeared in the NFL playoffs 25 times, have won 19 Division titles, 7 Conference championships, and a record 6 Super Bowl Championships.

The Pittsburgh Steelers are not the biggest nor do they have the financial resources of other NFL teams, but they are largely a family business that blossomed into greatness by embracing and investing in a philosophy of treating employees as family within a strong but flexible business model, as the organization set clear goals, gave clear direction, and mostly trusted in the talent it acquired to achieve success. Since 1969 the Rooney family, owners of the Steelers, has had only three head coaches for their team—Chuck Noll, Bill Cowher, and Mike Tomlin. They have not micromanaged the coaches; the coaches have, in turn, treated the players like adults, setting clear individual and team goals and high expectations for work, dedication, and behavior.

So how did this family-owned business, with no history of success, located in a blue-collar city with a struggling economy and a shrinking population, turn it around? They did it by selecting talent wisely, investing in that talent, modeling a philosophy and spirit of commitment and caring, and trusting that talent to perform to expectations. And while garnering success and being showered with rewards and accolades, the management treated those talented groups and individuals as if they truly mattered, were worthy adult professionals, were important, and counted. Sometimes this care was characterized with harsh realities of business and stark truthfulness, sometimes with tough love, but always with care and sensitivity to people. The Steelers didn't become successful by disregarding the sense and sensibilities of their people, but by recognizing that talent is both the most valuable and the most vulnerable asset.

The example of the Pittsburgh Steelers is a microcosm of the macrocosm of how successful organizations deal with the current global economic tsunami and stand tall and strong when this stressor is recent history. In tough times great companies and companies that aspire to be truly great, *built to last* if you will, seek ways to build and capitalize on competitive advantage. And they recognize that people can and will be the greatest component of advantage.

I hope I've at least begun to convince you of the importance of talent retention...in good times and bad. And if you have stuck with this "Introduction" so far, I suspect you see the value of my approach. Believe me, I've been around enough to see good times and bad, and over the course of my years in business, it's become clear to me that the companies that are successful in building large groups of committed and loyal workers, the best companies, the admirable companies, the companies with genuine *esprit de corps*, behave—in good times and bad!— in different ways than other organizations when it comes to handling the people they hire. As I watched and learned, I've recorded these behaviors and created tools, the "rules" referred to in the title, which virtually guarantee that the efforts, minds, and hearts of company's employees are focused on the corporate mission and challenged with producing outstanding results and competitive advantage.

This book describes these rules, and they are rules that any organization—large or small, high or low tech, public or private, for profit or not for profit—can apply to its own infrastructure and behavior pattern to cultivate a group of hard-working, productive, caring, committed, aligned, and engaged employees.

I must warn you that the list is long. Some rules are so logical and easy to apply that they might seem almost too simple to be of real value. Others are difficult to apply and take a major and sustained effort to incorporate—and positive outcomes take time to surface. All require serious commitment and the absence of "back sliding" to make a difference.

But, breathe easy, my friends, because here's something else I've learned from my interactions with stellar organizations that apply the rules scrupulously. To wit, although you must have an understanding and philosophical appreciation of all the rules, it is not necessary to apply every one of them, like following a recipe, to build a workplace that attracts and retains the best and most productive talent. Some rules are more easily adopted. Some provide more value to one organization than to another. Some require reallocating of resources; some are as simple as listening and being available. By and large, the ingestion of a "rules adoption cocktail" from what is advised in several of the chapters will go a long way to producing those committed employees. It can give your organization a running start; but remember, this is not a sprint—It's a marathon! Are you ready to run with the leaders? If so, join me, and those great companies, and turn the page.

—DFR

1

Understand Why Employees Come and Why They Stay

Check the calendar. The epoch of indentured servitude is long gone (as much as some executives I know want to bring it back!). Today, even in the midst of a historic economic downturn, your employees are not conscripts or servants. They are most likely volunteers. As much as you think your employees need you, that they are dependent on you, let's face it; the reverse is true. You are highly dependent on them for your success, your life style, and your living—now and into the future.

Oh, sure you can replace them, one after another, over a period of time, but you'll go broke. Your organization will be in ruins. Why? Well, some studies have shown that the cost to replace, retrain, and reintegrate a worker is more than one and a half times that lost worker's salary. Even then, as new employees come onboard, there are the hidden costs and intangible losses to your company from the rupture in cultural continuity and the transfer of institutional knowledge. (I beg you to keep this in mind, even as the national unemployment figure flutters near or into double digits.)

Is the picture starting to come into focus?

Let me put it another way. Your organization has assets, correct? Computers, source codes, real estate, equipment, customer lists, a valuable brand, and maybe even some cash. But do you know what the cumulative value of all those items is? Around 10 percent of your company's value. Max. That's because every day, at closing time, 90 percent of your assets walk out the door. Every day. And with luck, every morning, they volunteer to come back to work. Oh sure, in a short-term analysis, a few of your employees may say they are bound to you. They live paycheck to paycheck. They have mortgage payments due; they need the medical insurance; and they know they'd have a hard time finding other work. But how long do you think good, talented people stick around at places that treat them like draftees? Not long.

How do you keep them coming back? How do you keep good people from leaving, costing you one and a half times their salaries, and volunteering for your competitor's team? Well, what I am about to say may sound too simple to be important, too common to be common sense: *You engage them.* You engage them with a culture that boldly, publicly recognizes their value and binds their spirit to your company. And you have to work just as hard in bad times as in good times.

Let me take that up a notch, at the risk of sounding high-minded or theoretical. A culture of engagement inculcates and socializes your employees with a sense of—and reason for—genuine commitment to the organization. A culture of engagement also inspires individuals with a bias for action on the organization's behalf and pride. Yes, pride. I hope it is not news to you that a culture of engagement is important to the bottom line (*and* top line) of your company, because it is increasingly obvious that this is true, and authoritative surveys and studies affirm this again and again. Frankly, the stumbling block is to not recognize the importance of a caring, committed workforce to current and future success and competitive advantage. And the challenge is to determine the best ways to put the leadership behaviors and corporate infrastructure in place that enable that people-focused culture to emerge.

Note that I use the word *emerge*, because a culture of engagement cannot be imposed or implemented by edict or force of executive will. It is not a policy you write down on company handouts, like a vacation policy or instructions on how to fill out an expense report. But when it is place, and properly supported by the organization's leadership, it can and will bring forth the elusive quality called *employee discretionary effort*. Employees will offer that discretionary effort only when the aspirations of the organization and those of the employee are so in sync, aligned, that the employee—of his or her own initiative—takes great pride in going the extra mile and adding that extra dash of creativity and professionalism to achieve a professional goal that, lo and behold, builds the organization's wealth or dramatically advances its goals, as the employee learns, grows, and prospers.

Later in this chapter, I cite an example that highlights the beneficial economics of a culture of engagement. But for now, let's look at some steps you can take to establish a culture of engagement. The first step is for the executive leadership in the managers and leaders to recognize why their employees come to work. (Hint: Contrary to popular belief, it's not just about the money.) If you don't understand why people show up, why they *volunteer* at your workplace day after day, you miss an opportunity to attract people for why they *really* show up. It's no mystery. Here, too, research and valid polling data give us the same answer over and over again. First, people have a natural and inherent desire to make a contribution; to be a part of something larger than themselves, something of significance. Second, they want to do something that is worthwhile and notable; something they can be proud of—attach their names to. Third, they want to be recognized for their efforts and for the results. And fourth, they want all this to happen in an environment worthy of their efforts—a place that is respected and respectable.

See money on that list? No, it's not there.

Surprised?

Well, money is on the full list, but it's slotted into a subordinate position a little farther down. Make no mistake, people want to be compensated fairly for their work. But money is by no means the leading motivator for most of the talented, good people in today's workforce.

So, what brings people to work and keeps them there? It is a chance to do what they have been educated and trained to do at the highest level of success possible. Where they can grow and achieve, produce exemplary results, be recognized as worthy and special, and do it with others with similar talent, spirit, and professionalism for an entity that respects them and is worthy of high regard.

From Indentured Servants to Labor Unions: A History of Employer-Employee Relations

I know what you may be asking at this point: If research shows that the benefits of a culture of engagement are so beneficial to the top line, the bottom line, and the employees' well-being, then why haven't most companies implemented these policies? And why is it that in difficult business environments, nefarious companies use the economic downturn as an excuse to treat their employees worse?

Good questions, but they can be asked more productively at the causal level in this way: How have employers' relationships with their employees drifted into adversarial, and at time distrustful, circumstances? And how have those poor relations and lack of trust been embedded into policies and organizational design counter to the proper way to run a business? To answer that, take a brief look at the history of employer-employee relations.

It wasn't that long ago that the labor force migrated from an agrarian setting, in which most people worked outside of the cities in smaller groups, to an industrial urban setting. In industrial settings, jobs were centralized in factories, which were often situated in cities. At the risk of over oversimplifying a movement that took decades, even centuries, to act out, the golden rule that dictated employer-employee relations was this: He who had the gold made the rules. Typically in agrarian settings, people treated each other with a modicum of humanity, in which they shared risk, reward, responsibility and accountability. The industrial era disrupted that person-to-person dynamic. The main reasons were that employers had more than an ample supply of workers, and the tacit agreement to share between workers and employers wasn't actually very tacit after all, because employers dictated who worked, when they worked, and even *if* they worked. The employees had no power largely because they were interchangeable and could be summarily dismissed and replaced, at no actual cost to the employer.

Workers were not necessarily viewed or appreciated as persons and instead were valued largely for the capability of their production output. With replacement workers abundant, the workers needed, and deserved, no nurturing. They were de facto servants, bound by their need for work and by professional immobility. This historical context brings to mind Douglas McGregor's Theory X Management principle, which says people need to be controlled, pushed, and supervised by some management entity because unless that happens, workers won't produce. You need to threaten or entice workers to achieve production goals. As adversarial, counterproductive, and confrontational as the practice sounds today, it was a management style accepted as logical and brilliant for many years and still finds proponents in today's workplace.

Some cultural remnants of this type of employer-employee relationship were still in vogue as the way to succeed in business in the U.S. as late as the 1970s and 1980s. That's when organizations began to downsize, or "right size," as they reengineered themselves in response to activist shareholders' demands for higher levels of productivity, the push to maximize stakeholders' returns, and the scramble to conserve capital. Accompanying these changes in corporate structure was a change in the employer's perspective on people in the workplace. Until that time, organizational leadership often managed, pushed, and supervised the workers using Theory X Management. But as short-sighted as that was, it wasn't as harsh as it at first sounds, because along with the Theory X style came an implied social contract between employers and workers. It "promised" that if employees joined an organization, supported it with their labor, showed enduring loyalty, and parroted the company's mission as their own, the company promised virtual lifelong employment, a living wage with periodic increases, welfare benefits, time off for leisure, advancement opportunities, and a guaranteed post-retirement benefit. Baby boomers in the workplace bought wholesale into this arrangement. They were the children of the Depression and knew full well the value of long-term employment, supportive healthcare benefits, and guaranteed retirement income.

But in the 1970s and 1980s, organizations began to discover that this social contract was expensive. They realized that organizations could be consolidated, divested, and joined with others through acquisition that could deliver more bang for the buck and higher shareholder value. The ultimate result of this realization was that the social contract didn't just weaken, it disintegrated. Highly visible lay-offs occurred. What looked like cold-hearted directors of mergers and acquisitions (M&A) activity swept in and—without regard for loyalty or employees' work records—wiped out thousands of jobs and a great deal of good will. If you can sympathize with the shock and humiliation suffered by many of these workers, you can imagine the effect this treatment had on the families and especially the children of these workers who saw their parents golden years turned to brass.

What were the children of these workers doing? Well, these children of the baby boomers (many of them baby boomers themselves if they were born before 1964) were in the process of entering the work-force. If they were paying any attention to what happened to their parents, these children were sorely affected by these corporate decisions, and they were disillusioned. Moreover, many of them were determined to engage their future employers with a different kind of social contract, one that would give the worker more freedom and mobility.

The new social contract that came into being was much more circumspect, from both sides of the equation. Employers would never again offer the promise of lifelong work, nor incur the costs of that promise, but the "new breed" employees demanded access to resources, learning, and skills—acquired at the employer's expense—that were ultimately portable, in case the employees were even scuttled by the company or just decided to move on. This new breed of employees learned the lesson of the abandoned social contract very well.

Although the decreasing numbers of available skilled workers gave employers an incentive to train and keep employees (because they recognized the approaching struggle and costs to find and hire replacements), the employees' incentives to stay became more personal. Knowing that their employers were fully capable of cutting them loose at any time, in the interests of a few cents a share, these workers ran away from their part of the old social contract. They eschewed loyalty and dependence and readily replaced those with skills resting somewhere between feeling captured on one hand and blind loyalty on the other. They no longer felt captured because they were acquiring portable skills, and with a few job options in their back pockets, so to speak, they could take or leave a job. They were no longer capable of blind loyalty because they saw how their loyal parents had been treated poorly. Perhaps the most important employer-employee dynamic to emerge as a result of this tectonic shift in perspectives was that employees started examining exactly why they should stay anywhere, and employers started to examine what they could do to keep them.

Let's look at an analogy to understand this better because I recognize that it seems counter-intuitive. After all, I seem to be saying that employers should be training their employees for better jobs elsewhere. So, here goes. Do you know the difference between a **defined-benefit pension** and a **defined-contribution pension**? The defined-benefit pension promises what the pension will *pay out*, whereas the defined-contribution pension promises only what the employer will *put in*. A defined-contribution pension shifts the long-term onus from the employer to the employee because they are responsible for managing that pension for their own benefit.

Now, with that concept in mind, think of a new social contract between employers and their employees, one that has shifted the responsibility of lifelong employment from the employer to the employee, by simply defining what the organization is contributing to that employee in terms of training, tools, skills, and opportunity. The organization says that it is preparing the employee for lifelong employment but there are no guarantees—no defined payouts—for that employment. It's the *employees'* responsibility to nurture their own educational advancement and careers. Still, the employer has the onus of making the workplace a place where employees can make a contribution, do something worthwhile, work in an environment worthy of their efforts, and be recognized for what they do.

There is no doubt that this has shifted the power from the employer to the employee in many respects. but both sides of the equation have seen benefits. Employers have a heightened sense of how valuable employees are, and they see more clearly the benefit of investing in them, as they optimize the employee's productivity and create more profitable companies. Employees may have a little less trepidation about being laid off, because they have mobility with their skills and training, but—selfish as this may seem at first—they are always looking to the employer to help them get better at their jobs. If the employer can provide that training, and provide an engaged workforce that keeps employees happy, then everyone benefits, as the goals of the employer and employees are aligned. The employees' goals of wealth-building are in sync with the organization's, and with their goals in alignment, and the employees are naturally motivated to contribute their discretionary effort, creativity, and professionalism to advancement these shared goals.

A second piece of this employer-employee dynamic has to do with demographics. Baby boomers, the people born between 1946 and 1964, were the largest single group of people to enter into the workforce in American history. As they leave the workforce in the next 15 to 20 years, fewer people will replace them. In the harsh light of supply and demand—understanding that the situation won't last forever, and is actually just a blip—employers will have no choice but to engage employees, if they want to draw good people. Whereas baby boomers didn't have many choices, the children of baby boomers will.

They are less likely to "drink the Kool-Aid," so to speak, and they will be averse to working for a company that won't train them, give them tools to success, provide a great workplace, and recognize them for what they do.

Why People Work

Let's briefly revisit the reasons why people work. If you look at Maslow's hierarchy of human needs, one of the strongest needs is to be secure. But feeling secure isn't always just about money, because security can be expansively defined to include other things, such as safety and trust. So, first, accept the independence and culture of volunteerism that is the natural result of demographics and the changing nature of contemporary employer-employer relations. Note that security can be a residual effect, a natural consequence of today's employer-employer dynamic. With security assured, people naturally look to the next level of hierarchy of human needs, relationships. Employee want a place to work in which their contribution and workplace relationships are socially acceptable; a workplace in which employees are proud to talk about with their friends; a place that enables them to walk through life with their heads held high. With that assurance, the employee looks even farther down the list of Maslow's hierarchy: the need to be recognized. Security and the desire to be employed someplace that garners respect are two needs that are easy to understand. But just as universal and essential is the need to be recognized.

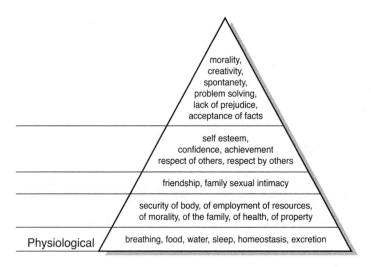

Figure 1.1

This is one reason why Bill Gates still works, why Warren Buffet and Steve Jobs come to work. There is just no denying the importance of ego and no shame in acknowledging that it is basic human need to want some strokes now and then. No matter how wealthy you are, you want to be recognized for what you have contributed, and if you can offer that in a workplace where you feel secure and are proud to work, then you are well on your way to engaging employees and eliciting from them that thing that they give only to people and organizations that treat them with respect and value their contribution: *extraordinary effort.*

Because we are working through Maslow's hierarchy of human needs, let's look farther down the list. We have covered security, and the need to be recognized. Next, you can't ignore the importance of relationships and the role that relationships play when building a sense of workplace camaraderie. Please don't dismiss workplace camaraderie are unimportant or frivolous, because camaraderie isn't about wasting time in the lunchroom or hanging around the water cooler talking about golf or sports. It is a major contributor to why people come to work. Fostering camaraderie is ultimately about productivity, and its importance has been heightened in the workplace only by the changing the nature of the family, especially since the end of World War II.

How has the changing dynamic of the American family affected workplace camaraderie? Believe me, it is less of a stretch than you think. Here's why. When I grew up, I was no more than a 5-iron shot from the homes of my nearest relatives, and we gathered often. Every Sunday, the entire family sat down and ate together. My grandparents, my aunts and my uncles, we all sat down on a weekly basis. In American today, other than the people who live under your roof, on average, Americans live more than 120 miles away from their closest relative. The nuclear family is no longer the central social unit of American life. Yet the breakdown of the nuclear family hasn't changed that humans are social beings. So, the family needs to be replaced with something, some social unit. And that social unit is the workplace. People come to work to be at their social club—it's not a party club but a social club, a place for quality human interaction among people they know and trust. If that social club is supportive, allows people to trust one another, and has high camaraderie, that's not only what draws people to come to work each day, it's what makes them stay. So, when designing corporate infrastructure whose aim is to create a culture of engagement, it's imperative that you recognize the core position played by the work social club. Ignore it at your own peril.

I hope by now you can see the interrelated nature of the core elements and core requirements for engaging a workforce. Employees want to make a contribution while doing something worthwhile. They want to do this in a place worthy of their efforts. They want to be recognized for what they do, they want to work in a place with high camaraderie, and they want to work in a place where there is a high level of trust and respect. We haven't covered trust and respect yet, so let's close this chapter by focusing on them. Although these are the last items covered in this chapter about why employees come to work and why they stay, trust and respect are no less important than the previously introduced concepts

A core element of what makes employees stay at a job—and remember that all your employees are volunteers—is their trust in the organization and the respect the organization expresses to the employees (or that the organization helps engender from coworkers). This social exchange isn't difficult to grasp; I am sure you have experienced it in other areas of your life. If the organization believes in the employees and trusts them to do good work—and expresses that trust through the investment in career development, training, advancement opportunity, and availability to resources—*surprise!* The employees take that seriously and return the favor by trusting the organization. The employees allow the organization to make the decisions to propel the business forward; they also trust that the organization has the best interests of the employees in mind with every decision. With that trust, there is less cynicism because the goals of the organization and the goals of the employees are in sync. The more the organization succeeds, the more the employees succeed. It's a self-feeding cycle that accelerates and becomes more effective when more people commit to it from both sides of the equation.

2

Play "Win-Win" with Your Employees (and Allow Them to Be All They Can Be—for Self and Company)

Business leaders at every level must build a work environment that enables each employee's **preferred self** to emerge at the workplace through an alignment and balance of the employee's personal attributes and needs with the organization's goals.

Sounds a little academic and even Mary Poppins-ish, doesn't it, this talk of *preferred self*? It's a term that even seems to lapse over into— arghhh!—guru or consultant's speak! But a *preferred self* is something that's literal and a part of the opportunity for workplace productivity, and it's a state of being that you have probably experienced—at work, at home, or more likely at play—though you may have called it by another name that's easy to describe but hard to explain. (I say all of this mindful that some readers will contest whether the downturn in the economy even affords us any latitude for seemingly touchy-feely approaches to managing people. But I assure you, what I'm talking about is ultimately all about the bottom line.)

A noted workplace researcher at Carnegie Mellon University, Denise Rousseau, found, and I concur, that an employee's preferred self is the work-self you are comfortable with when working free of the facades and defenses people erect to protect themselves from the inconsistent behaviors of leaders or the organization.

21

I am sure you know when your preferred self *isn't* allowed to emerge. That's when you hear workplace phrases such as, "I've never seen a more highly charged political workplace environment," or "This place is toxic." Heard that before?

In that workplace scenario, you feel defensive, on guard, and you spend more time protecting your back than getting anything done. But when the preferred self emerges and an employee can spend her creative energy focusing on doing, building, creating, completing, and accomplishing, (instead of watching her back), then that person is acting and working in a **maximum comfort zone**. That's an employee who feels good about what he is doing, how he is doing it, *and* how he and his work is perceived. When those stars align, that employee can be completely authentic to coworkers, simultaneously vulnerable and trusting.

This isn't a sing-Kumbaya-around-the-campfire moment I am talking about; it's not some workplace epiphany, when the world turns to slow motion as people smile at each other in mystical contentment. This is a time of peak productivity! And who couldn't use a little more of that in our current economic predicament? This is a time when the employee's self-interest and the aspirations of the organization are mostly in sync and great things get done.

For an artist or an athlete, a preferred self might be easier to attain and much easier to see than for an individual within an organizational infrastructure. That's because the artist's and athlete's "occupations," *per se*, are based in individual performance, and the infrastructure is just his identity. If you were to introduce that individual performer into an organizational structure—even if it were an organization of artists working creatively and collaboratively—the demand of organizational infrastructures and the stressors of the workplace have the potential to drain the joy out of work, no matter how much creativity is required to make it. There's a simple reason for that—and a slew of tactics to counter it. Let's look a little deeper.

When an organization starts focusing on, well, *organizing*, they are not focused on joy. *Joy?* That's another term that may be a little too touchy-feely. Would it still seem so touchy-feely if I were to directly correlate workplace joy with productivity? And joy with the bottom line? And joy as an essential key to creating mind-blowing innovation and breakout new products?

After all, do you think products like the iPod were created in an atmosphere of drudgery? Do you think GPS devices were designed by people who burned with singular resentment in their lonely cubicles, as they plotted revenge? New miracle drugs concocted by people who hated their coworkers and dreamed of escaping their desks? The elegant curves of a 740Li series BMW made by people who dread getting out of bed in the morning?

Of course not!

An organizational infrastructure that enables a worker's preferred self to joyously emerge creates the most profitable and innovative workplaces, with staggeringly high rates of employee retention—four to five times the industry average.

Yes, it's true. I've been there to see it, in good times and in bad. I know what helped to make it happen and helped sustain it.

A great organization creates supportive workplace environments in which preferred selves can come to the surface. But it's more than just providing a person with a task he likes to do. The truth is that any employee might get satisfaction for doing a worthwhile task, with access to the right resources and team. However, preferred self can emerge only when the workers see that they are contributing to something bigger than themselves. They must recognize, and be reminded on a regular basis, what part they play in the overall success of the organization. The individual worthwhile task is exponentially more important to the individual (and the organization) if the employees sees it as part of a grander plan to which they are making an integral contribution. And the "illusive effort" you are always seeking in your employees—that burst of creativity and contribution that gives you iPods, GPS invention, miracle drugs, and great machines? It will be produced voluntarily by the employee's preferred self.

Does this mean that the workplace must provide an endless series of ecstatic moments? No, you can't run a workplace like that any more than you can run a relationship or a friendship like that. It would be ruinous and exhausting. But you do need to create infrastructure (physical, emotional, and organizational) in which an environment can emerge that lets people do what they love to do, while tapping into their personal willingness to perform. That environment must also have a system in place to recognize and reward what these people do.

What I recommend has nothing to do with the size of the company. Or even the financial resources of the organization. Or even the sector of the economy in which a company operates. When I speak to groups about this topic, inevitably a person from a small company asks, "We're such a small company; how is this possible?" Or "How can you justify that when we're struggling to just survive." The next day, I'll hear someone ask, "We're such a large company; how is this possible?" Or "Why do we need that when everyone understands that we try to stay competitive and keep afloat?"

But the job of management and leadership is to take people in *any* size group and—without impeding their progress with a difficult infrastructure—allow the enlightened self-interest of the worker to thrive, and drive productivity, whenever it advances the organization's overall goals and profitability.

That said, it isn't easy to achieve. It's not necessarily expensive, but it takes commitment. Serious commitment. All the way up and down the ladder. In fact, allowing the preferred self to emerge isn't just a matter of day-to-day operations, though that is part of it. It's an **acculturation** process that must influence every aspect of the company's operations, from nurturing and retaining employees all the way down to the plans for the holiday party. And it even extends into the recruiting process. That's because the culture that enables an employee's preferred self to emerge is one that will draw the right people to your organization, people who are eager to work in positive and productive environments, people who want to be part of great efforts.

Make no mistake, the proper environment acts as a beacon that calls the right kind of people to you. So, part of building that acculturation is having a clear understanding of the kinds of employees that you want, the kinds of people who will propel your organization forward *and* the kind of leadership you need to attract them. As a baseline requirement, that includes recognizing the employees and candidates with the kinds of skills and attitude required to fuel the **productivity propulsion mechanism** of the preferred-self work environment.

Let's look at a real-world example. Take a widely known company such as Starbucks. Starbucks believes that the way to get exceptional performance and productivity from people and management teams is to have an environment focused on trust. It believes that the trust factor has at least five elements. First, Starbucks believes that you need to build an infrastructure that enables people to take risks, without fear of career-debilitating punishment if the risks bring failure. Second, Starbucks makes its people accountable, not just responsible, but accountable. (There's a difference.) Third, they trust that the people understand good service. Fourth—related to element number three— it believes that when people understand good service, they will be creative when delivering it. And fifth, Starbucks trusts that its people will pass on these beliefs and practices when new people come on board. That corporate infrastructure—when clearly and consistently communicated and acted on by everyone at every station in the company— will serve not only as a guiding light for current employees, but it also acts as a way to draw the kind of people who want to work on this corporate culture. Even though I have never worked at Starbucks, I can recognize people in the world who would flourish there, because it is a place in which a preferred self can emerge that is gregarious, creative, service-oriented, and customer-focused. I can also recognize a good number of people who would not flourish there, and whose engagement with the company would be a costly waste of time.

How is this preferred–self culture communicated? Well, here's the overall message: We are building and trying to sustain a workplace in which you as an individual will be respected and nurtured as long as you respect and nurture others. But communicating it starts with emphatic and determined leadership that lays down what it values as a company. Second, that leadership must put forth a three-, five-, and ten-year mission that identifies awesome goals that it will accomplish. Third, the leadership must create a model of behavior—from the top down—that provides an environment filled with respect, trust, recognition, and excellence, an environment that plans to engage employees with growth opportunity as it leverages their skills, intellects, and aspirations to build corporate wealth. By communicating those things, the leadership has taken giant steps on its paths to find people who at least aspire to fit into that kind of environment. If you go forward living up to those values and goals, and that behavior model, what you get is a workforce that is filled with valued, engaged people who take responsibility for the company's success, people who have the attitude that they will give until it hurts—though it never really hurts—people who have their bodies and their souls involved in the task of the workplace.

Now I know that you might be one of those people who are used to rewarding short-term gains. That's typical of short-term, bottom-line focused management theory and practice. I think many executives think that rewarding short-term goals is the only way to drive productivity, and this approach to business is especially tempting in the economic downturn. Anything else would be looked at as being soft. Well, there is nothing wrong with being tough. So, when I am talking about the preferred self, I'm not saying that you can bring it out only with family picnics and circles of singing employees. Preferred-self environments are *only* about win-win-win. The employees win; the company wins; the customer wins. The owners win; the stakeholders (shareholders) win. The company makes gains as a result of the employees' efforts, yet the employees grow as well through learning and professional develop and they become better people, better employees, better contributors than they were last year because of the growth and development that the employer made available to them. As a result, the organization and its products and services are more valuable. And there is no embarrassment in success, because, yes, the company is making money on the backs of the employees' efforts, but the employees aren't being beaten down as the company succeeds.

With that in mind, let's take a look at what kind of people do you need for this type of workplace environment. It varies by organization, by the texture of the enterprise. A person who works well in pharmaceuticals might not work in a tech startup. Retail customer service drives some people crazy, yet they might flourish in an educational environment or a manufacturing setting. One thing that remains true across the spectrum of various organizations is that the right good people always should have the requisite skills (a baseline requirement, a given) along with a capacity to grow and develop, and an intellectual and visceral understanding of the organization's goals. They must see that their personal advancement is not adversarial to the organization's advancement. The organization's leadership must hold the same opinion; indeed, the advancement and success of the individuals and the organization should be in sync.

Too often organizations hire people with great track records but who are not a good fit for engaging themselves and a preferred-self environment. When I interview candidates during the recruitment and hiring process (collectively referred as the **onboarding process**), I look for people who are interested in being part of something larger than themselves, people who are interested in joining a team. I also look for people who are naturally curious about where the company is going, how it got to where it is today, and what opportunities it offers them. For that last item, that might seem odd that I welcome that inquiry. I don't find it selfish when someone essentially asks, "What's in it for me?" Because in the right setting, *what's in it for them* is *what's in it for the company*, and there you'll find an alignment of personal and corporate ambitions.

Now let's dig a little deeper into how to draw the right good people. As your culture acts as a beacon to potential new hires, you will draw people who think they fit the model and say, "That's the right place for me." Let me give you another example. There is a company in semi-rural Pennsylvania called Minitab. It's a large statistical analysis company that runs a great shop. Minitab is close to Penn State, with a high quality of life, with a highly developed intellectual culture. Minitab prides itself on creating a workplace environment that is highly communicative, caring, and nurturing. Their people do indeed aspire to intellectual excellence and hard work. In its Pennsylvania location, near Penn State, the local environment is appropriate for the personal needs of its ideal employees. People come to Minitab to do interesting and challenging work in a competitive environment, and they live in a local culture that is loaded with activities and events that interest them. So, the Minitab brand attracts people who fit. But perhaps more important, from the bottom-line side of the equation, Minitab knows who won't fit. During the interview process, it does not need to guess that a prospect will be a good employee and can clearly identify the people who won't fit in. If candidates come to Minitab thinking how fun it would be to live near Penn State but are interested in a stratified workplace and a system that rewards superstars, then they won't fit there. Minitab can pick them out and remove them from the hiring process before any further engagement gets expensive. If candidates are curious about deeply engrained attributes of the organization, that's a good sign. It's also a good sign if they have done research on the history of the company and its place in the community. Those kinds of people will have a natural affinity for Minitab. However, if people take time during the interview to talk about bonuses, salary, while asking about the gym, and the pool, that's not a good sign. You see, the corporate culture is so clearly defined at Minitab, that even during the recruiting and hiring process, it looks for other members of its tribe and know them when it sees them.

Let me give you another real-world example. When I was vice president of human resources at SAS Institute, we started to offer low-cost daycare to our employees at the North Carolina campus. We wanted to offer this perk to our employees because it treated them well, and at another level it helped with employee productivity and was therefore cost-effective. We also did it to send a beacon to the community that clearly said that we were a company that recognized the value and importance of family to our employees, and that we cared enough for them to make it available. It not only kept good people, but it also drew the right good people to us.

Want to see how something like that actually pays off? Here's an example: When I was at SAS Institute years ago, we were interviewing for a high-level technology position. A young man from California sent a resume that looked great. So, we brought him in. He interviewed well and was a great fit. So, we made him an offer, which he accepted. When I did my post-hire interview, I told him that we typically had difficulty attracting technically gifted people from the west coast to North Carolina. I asked him what drew him to SAS Institute. He said it was the daycare that stood out. I asked him, "So how old are your kids." He said he didn't have any kids. I asked him, "Kid's on the way?" "No." So, I asked how long he'd been married?" He said, "I'm not married. I'm not even in a serious relationship." "Then why," I asked, "did the daycare draw you here?" He said that a company that expressed its concern for the well being of its employees and their families by offering them daycare was a place he'd like to work. He felt the fit.

So you see that looking for the right people is all part of an over arching plan, a multi-pronged approach that first draws and hires people for their skills and talent. These are the people who make your organization competitive. These are the people who have the potential for capabilities growth. Yet they must fit into the organization's preferred-self culture, people who fit into not only *what* you are but also *how* you operate. However, if you bring on people who are all potential, yet have no talent and skills, then you risk poisoning the workplace atmosphere by dragging along someone who was hired *just* for their potential. Others will look over the cubical wall and say, "Hey, this guy's not pulling his weight!" Third, if you hire someone who has talent, and ambition, but they are not a good cultural fit—they are not team players, or they are selfish without giving back—the "wisdom of the crowd" at work will feel as though the integrity of the group has been dragged down.

Well, with all this talk of talent, skills, potential aptitude, and fit, you know I had to come up with a sports metaphor sooner or later. Right? Here's a good one: Alex Rodriguez. Since his first full season in 1996 through 2007, he has put up, shall we say, some fairly good numbers. He leads the majors in home runs, runs scored, RBIs, and total bases and extra-base hits. Of all players in baseball history prior to their 31st birthday, Alex Rodriguez is first all-time in home runs, runs scored and total bases; second in extra base hits and RBI, and fourth in hits, tainted somewhat now with recent revelations. He is the youngest player ever to hit 500 home runs, breaking a record set in 1939. He is, by any other description, a superstar and one of the finest athletes to ever walk the planet. (He was recruited to the University of Miami as a baseball player and as a quarterback!)

He currently has a 10-year contract with the Yankees, worth $275 million, with a $30 million bonus if he breaks the all-time home run record (762). But when the Yankees signed him away from the Texas Rangers, there was a great uproar about whether he would fit. He surely had the talent and aptitude, but Rodriguez took the position of third base. The position of shortstop, his traditional spot, was already taken by the beloved Derek Jeter. At third base, Rodriguez was not a golden glover. And he took the position probably for less than market value than if he went to be a shortstop on another team. The reason?

He felt that the Yankees were about winning championships, and he wanted to contribute—even at some relative sacrifice—to something larger than himself. He even changed his number to 13 from his life-long number 3, because 3 was already retired in honor of a man named Babe Ruth.

Will he be the next Mr. Yankee? Or achieve the status and charisma of Derek Jeter? Maybe so. But in spite of the money, he showed a sense of humility to achieve something that he is interested in, and it was aligned with something George Steinbrenner wants. For Rodriguez it wasn't about him, but about "us." And in the long run, as he develops professionally at the Yankees, their faith in him and his faith in them will likely earn everyone far more money over time than if he has gone from team to team as a gun-for-hire hot-shot, achieving sugar highs here and there but not contributing to an enduring team legacy.

Are you hiring people like Alex Rodriguez, with superstar qualities, great potential, and an achievement-filled resume that want to be part of a team? Are you drawing people to your organization like that West-Coast software engineer who wanted to work at SAS Institute because of the company's philosophy about the value of people, even though he didn't plan to take advantage of it? You need to recognize a member of your tribe during the hiring process and confidently turn away people who won't fit. Can you?

3

Cultivate Leadership, Not Management, and Know the Difference!

I'm not one for didactic, nonnegotiable statements of fact, but I'm going to risk one here. The reason? The science of management is quite well known, and the difference between managers and leaders is clear. So here goes: Managers direct and control; they deploy, coordinate, delegate, and manipulate resources. But managers are not necessarily leaders. Whereas managers administrate, leaders have the power to *influence*, to *motivate*, even *inspire*, and those are distinctly different traits. Indeed, true leadership is the ability to display attributes that make people want to follow.

Whereas managers can be provincial, selective, even guarded, leaders are inclusive, passionate, and express an expansive vision. Whereas managers push people forward, true leaders take action and look over their shoulders to find legions following them and emulating their action. In fact, true leaders somehow naturally, and without fanfare or plan, behave as a role model and allow their behavior to be modeled by peers, subordinates, and employees. If leaders are open, authentic, communicative, and supportive without being paternal, that spirit can more easily pervade the entire enterprise and can even make great leaders out of great managers. Let's take a closer look.

All too commonly, leadership is characterized by a "teachable point of view." A leader has a perspective that he articulates, teaches, or proscribes; people who follow that leader absorb that point of view and apply it to a desired outcome. However, my own perspective is that leaders shouldn't pigeonhole or limit themselves into the role of teacher. Instead, they should aim to provide a leadership style that *engages* rather than proscribes. A look at the history of management theory can give you some insights here.

The classic approach to defining management comes from the days of "scientific management," and its lead theorist, Frederick Winslow Taylor. who died in 1915. Taylor was originally a mechanical engineer, and he tried to bring the lessons learned from mechanical efficiency into the world of industrial efficiency and the management of people. He is sometimes referred to as the "father of scientific management," and he had four key principles, called **Taylor's Principles**. Briefly, they are

1. Replace rule-of-thumb methods with methods based on a scientific study.
2. Scientifically select, train, and develop each employee.
3. Provide detailed instruction and supervision of each worker.
4. Let managers apply scientific management principles to planning the work; let workers perform the tasks.

Sound like a guy you'd like to have over for dinner? Well, I am sure he'd be an interesting guest, though maybe a little strict around the topic of table manners and which fork you should use first. Seriously, his point is that management should be focused on control and delegation. But my point is that this style of management doesn't have anything to do with leading people or engaging employees. To truly engage people, you must have employees who *think as owners*. And these four Taylor Principles treat employees merely as pawns in a scheme whose action are to be measured and improved upon as though they were machines or robots. And it's hard to get that illusive extra effort out of a robot. They do merely what they are programmed to do; they don't stay late because they are passionate about their jobs.

Let's focus a little more closely on what makes a good manager, and then look at how managers can grow into leaders.

The first thing that good managers need to understand is that any attempt to engage or any attempt to facilitate positive outcomes for an organization now requires management to act as an agent of developing and retaining talent. It's not enough to just maximize the efficiency of employees in the Frederick Winslow Taylor model. The manager shouldn't be a director and supervisor but instead serve as a primary resource for knowledge, services, and facilities that employees need to do what is asked and expected. Sounds easy, right? But we're talking way beyond resources and budgets. A good manager should serve as a remover of impediments, a resource that offers a broad perspective and institutional knowledge in service to help employees do their jobs.

Are you with me, or are you too worried about the economic recovery? Because I am going to push this a little further and show how great managers become leaders. In the previous chapter, and elsewhere in this book, we focus on creating environments in which an employee's *preferred self* can emerge. Well, good managers use their authority and autonomy in ways that allow their employees' *preferred selves* to emerge and avoid the politics, process, bureaucracy, and circumstantial matters that traditionally get in the way of executing a plan.

As managers develop into leaders, they encourage when things are going well, consent to prudent risk taking, and—in the end—act like quarterbacks. A game plan is in place, which the leadership created, and the quarterback's job is to communicate what each player is expected to do to achieve results. Then, the quarterback basically takes the objective, hands it off, and allows people to do their jobs. But to be fully effective, a quarterback must manage the huddle and get the team to believe in the game plan. That's where leadership comes in. There are characteristics of manager-leaders that bring out the "players" engagement and calls forth their discretionary effort. Let's look closer at those leadership characteristics.

To capture the hearts and minds of your employees as a leader, how do you behave? Well, first, leaders are passionate. They express the passion about the task at hand; they sell the worthiness of the task and its level of importance; they understand and communicate the greatness of winning; and they are fully engaged. Also, all good leaders have vision. They can envision the end result and express that vision in what they say and how they behave. They have high levels of energy for the work, which is infectious, and they motivate people who want to emulate the leader's character. Leaders are inclusive, too. They know that every member on the team is a valued contributor, from the superstar engineer all the way down to the person who turns the last bolt on the finished product. They know that no employees should be observers of a process but engaged participants in it, and they make clear to the employees that each plays an essential role. To go back to the football analogy: A crisp pattern run by a tight end who was never supposed to get the ball in the first place will draw defenders away from the *real* ball carrier on that play and facilitate the game plan.

Leaders are also not just observers. They have dirty nails, knees, and elbows. They can't be dispassionate and don't mind jumping in to get a taste of what's going on. When leaders serve as resources, they are not just being smart, though that never hurts. Instead, they are placing resources and responsibility in the hands of people along with some autonomy to execute. They share knowledge, but they also facilitate knowledge sharing, as they recognize that they don't have all the answers. They use the wisdom of their experience and skill to add value to the organization's processes, and they use their perspective to help each group take the blinders off, to focus externally, not myopically.

Another leadership characteristic is openness, and that requires *active listening*. Leaders recognize that they might not be the smartest person on campus, and that in most cases—and this is central—*none of us* is as smart as *all of us*. They are open to diverse points of view and alternative ways to complete tasks. That openness allows for bad news to be delivered quickly—in either direction, up or down the ladder—and for problems to be addressed and solved directly.

Leaders are also externally focused. They have the perspective to recognize that the organization is ultimately all about the customers and product excellence, whether the leader is managing a multifacility hospital complex, a 500-member software development team, or a startup with 10 employees. They see that the products or service created is not about "us," per se, but about focusing outward in the competitive world of commerce.

Leaders require some measure of charisma. I don't mean charm and personally. In fact, I don't even think that leaders should have to know the names of everyone in the company. But one of the characteristics of leadership I previously alluded to is that the leader should practice behavior that can—and should—be emulated throughout the enterprise. If leaders knows just the names, aspirations, and concerns of the people around them, then those managers, in turn, are given a kind of subtle mandate and a behavior model to know the people they work with in the same way. In this manner, the behavior is passed down the line. If managers are gruff and dismissive, cold and impersonal, that's the behavior model that will be emulated by their subordinates, and they will model that behavior along the command chain.

Leaders should cultivate a personal presence that people want to be around. That doesn't mean that they should be standup comics, or saccharine sweet; they can't be someone who gives out hugs while delivering coffee to everyone's desk each morning. But leaders should smile more than they frown; leaders are empathetic in an adult way, rather than being sympathetic in a maternal or paternal way. In short, leaders care and show that they care. They create workplace environments in which employees can develop a sense of trust and caring.

Leaders must display courage and visibly show that courage at crucial times, as when—such as today—the economy forces some tough decisions. How is this expressed in a literal, practical way? It's simple: For starters, leaders should talk about "the elephant in the room." They should address problems directly through imperative, decisive, effective action. Good leaders don't remain silent when they see something that's wrong or misguided. Remember, your organization is going to emulate the leaders' actions, and by demonstrating at the top that your organization is one that addresses and solves problems, this culture of problem solving becomes part of the organization's culture. And it makes everyone feel invested in the organization, because they feel as though they can change it. In a recent book . Geography of Bliss, the author Eric Weiner points out that Switzerland is one of the happiest places on Earth. One of the reasons is that they vote as often as seven times a year. How does it make them happy? The average citizen is not locked out of the political process, and there is no sense that an elite class of people is making decisions. Average citizens can affect the process if they want to add their voice. So instead of low levels of enragement, there is a sense of engagement. The citizens are treated as *owners*. Now, think of that in terms of employees. Imagine how much rage/discontent/ boredom can build up if the employees do not see themselves having a voice/input/sweat equity/intellectual capital in the results produced by the organization, if they don't feel engaged or part of the organization's processes. On the contrary, imagine how engaged employees feel if they "voted" in some way such as the Swiss, if they had some ownership in the direction and outcomes of their organization...even if that "say" were expressed not by binding votes, but just the knowledge and comfort, along with accountability, that exists in which the leaders encouraged, respected, and genuinely responded to "employee-constituents."

As leaders ask the tough questions, talk about the "elephant in the room," the obvious truths, and engage employees in discussions in a genuine open way, they are also free to engage in genuinely difficult discussions about performance, results, process, and workplace politics. In that case, this is a conversation with the employees and *not* a gripe session in which everyone boils over with frustration and resentment because the problems have gone on too far. With this approach, the appraisal of the organization can be handled in an adult, nonjudgmental manner. When there is open communication and issues are not buried or hidden, it's a win-win for leadership and employees. There is no zero sum game in which everything that leadership grabs is kept away from employees and vice versa; in fact, the communication can be remarkably nonadversarial. And anything that is gained from either side is simultaneously a bounty for both, because there actually aren't two sides. Everyone is an owner.

Does all of this sound like a tall task? Well, keep reading, because I am not yet done. I think you see that point, though. Leading is a demanding task, and though some people are born to the task and intuitively understand what I am describing in this chapter, these traits can be learned and perfected.

Because leaders act in such a way that their behavior can be emulated throughout the organization, leaders must also be accountable. When leaders are accountable, even at the highest level, it sends a message to their peers and subordinates that the leaders knows how to accept credit and absorb guilt. It also allows the leaders to disperse credit in an authentic manner, and hold peers and subordinates accountable, accordingly. So, by accepting responsibility and accountability, leaders gain points or credit, per se, to dispense worthy, authentic praise, and direct criticism and to distribute rewards and wealth.

Look at it this way, when a great coach loses a game, in the post-game press conference he usually says, "We played awfully." He is applying blame; at the same time he allows the team to accept blame. That's a culture of humility, accountability, and calm adult discourse, and if the coach is saying things like that publicly to the national press, you can bet he expects that same humility, accountability, and calm adult discourse among his players. They are, after all, owners of the victories—and the defeats.

Does mean these leaders must be soft? Hardly. When one of Vince Lombardi's players was asked, "Does Vince play favorites?" The player answered. "No, he treats us all equally, like dogs." Yet Lombardi was trusted for his consistency and for his ability to bestow praise and criticism with equal power and affect. And he had the respect of every player who played on his teams. He made people want to follow.

4

Provide Ample and Appropriate Resources

I still remember when my dad first handed over the keys to the family car. I suspect you remember a similar event in your life as well. Whichever relative or friend was part of that "passage" ceremony, I bet you saw it as much more than just the chance to get behind the wheel solo for the first time. The keys were a vote of trust, and if your dad was like my dad, the keys were handed over with an eye-to-eye look that said more than words could convey: *Here's the car, now justify my trust in you by acting responsibly and doing the right thing.* It could well be that I am alive and kicking today because his trust in me was well-founded.

That said, if his handoff of the keys had been accompanied by a strict and stern lecture, or the threat of punishment for the slightest infraction, or a diatribe about exactly how an automobile is to be driven, believe me, I may well have rewarded his lack of faith with defiance, a measure of recklessness, and maybe even spite. Instead, that calm, adult conveyance of the car keys was also a conveyance of calm, adult-to-adult expectations, as much as it was a vote of confidence that I'd do the right thing.

Now, in the context of the workplace, think of the car as a training resource, a state-of-the-art tool, financial assets, or even the reputation of product, service, or the company itself. Next, think of this story in the sense of a manager or leader handing over "the keys" to an employee or subordinate. And let's assume that those keys can open up budgetary resources or tool sets, or access to a team of talented people. When conveyed in the right spirit, that act of handing over the keys is nothing short of a vote of trust and confidence in the employee or subordinate. It's an act that says: *Here's the power and the resources, now, justify my trust in you to act responsibly and do the right thing.* If the handover is accompanied by a strict lecture, threats, suspicion, and a lack of trust, there's a fair chance that you would return the favor and out of spite (yes, even reasonable adults are capable of spite) "reward" that lack of faith with resentment, imprudence, and maybe even a subliminal urge to bring the entire effort down around you—the classic lose-lose outcome. And you can imagine some of the thoughts that would be raised during this exchange, the kindest being, "If you treat me like a child, I'll act like a child." The human, emotional dynamic of these two interactions isn't all that different in either situation; only the context has changed.

In organizations, resources are a three-tined fork, a trident of sorts. You want your staff to be successful, but it's up to them to choose the path to that success. That's one tine. Second, the conveying of resources and control to employees can indicate how you feel about them (either positive or negative). Done properly with the right good people, it can indicate that the employee is important and that the organization values her judgment and potential for contribution. The third tine is that handing over the control of resources to someone inextricably links that person to the success (or failure) of the project, and it can motivate them to take ownership of the project and to invest pride and extra effort in doing it well. When you convey power, resources, and control to someone, that employee will say, "They believe in me. They want me to be successful, and I have to show them that I am worthy of that respect; I will justify that trust, and I will make something of these resources."

As to what resources you should provide, that's the task of managers and leaders to decide. But let me tell you something: As you start to appraise what resources are required don't put your people on starvation diets or burnout budgets. To keep employees engaged, first you have to give them the proper tools and resources. To put it crassly, you can't give someone a knife and send them to a gun fight. Don't hand someone a hammer and ask him to make a fine sculpture. Accordingly, don't put your people on a strict diet just because they are demonstrating *esprit de corps*, and you know the team will put up with it because they have pride and drive. That only stresses and fatigues your people.

Second, you have to realize that resources aren't always about money and materials. Sometimes it's about team members who are shrewdly chosen. Sometimes it's a matter of aligning resources with desired outcomes and expressing how you—as managers and leaders of the organization—expect the resources to be prudently used. But it couldn't be plainer: Adequate tools and resources are not only essential to tactical success, they signal to employees that you think they have the discretion required to allocate the organization's resources and authorize their deployment.

When you have this kind of employee-manager dynamic taking place, and the employees (*and* manager *and* leaders) are all acting as owners, the allocation of proper resources serves an even higher purpose. It also announces the high expectations the organization has for the success of an initiative. Remember if you will, the biblical Parable of the Talents. A wealthy merchant gave each of his three servants "talents" (portions of his assets) each according to his ability to care for while he was away on a journey. One servant received five and using his skills and efforts doubled it to ten. A second servant was given two talents and through his initiative turned those two into four. The third servant had received one talent, but buried the talent to hide it and protect it from harm. So when the merchant returned the servant presented the one talent to him unscathed. The first and second servants were praised and rewarded because they had used their skills and enthusiasm to build on the assets of their leader. The third servant was censured—with weeping and gnashing of teeth, no less— because he hadn't lived up to the trust and confidence the merchant had in him to do good for himself and the business. (Maybe the merchant didn't properly convey his expectations.) As I am sure you have guessed by now, you want your employees and subordinates to behave as the first and second servants had done. You want them to take the resources and invest the work, sweat, and pride to make something out of them. But as this parable also makes clear from what it does not say, you need for your employees and subordinates to have a clear idea of your expectations of improving the situation; you don't want them protectively burying resources and returning just your initial investment. You want them to bring back something twofold or greater.

Let's take this out of the clouds, away from the metaphors and down to earth. Imagine how a software developer or salesperson must feel about his job, company, and opportunity when he is left to struggle to succeed with out-of-date information, tools, or technology. Do you think he feels honored and valued? Is he excited about the task ahead? Of course not. And do you think those feelings are expressed in the effort delivered and the results? They are. By depriving or limiting resources for your people, you signal disregard, indifference, even disrespect for them and a lack of importance for the work you ask them to do. At some level, those "messages" result in poor or marginal performance and less than the desired results. The failure to provide appropriate resources is an indication to workers of how the organization treats *everything* it is supposed to value—products, customers, and people.

Now, this is not to say that companies that do not have the finances to spend on supportive resources should put themselves out of business to live up to this rule. But each company that wants to hire, develop, and keep a committed and productive work force, *must* do everything with its means to provide appropriate resources.

The next logical question is how and when do you convey the expectations that accompany the resources? If the merchant in the parable failed at anything, it was certainly his laissez-faire handling of giving instructions. He was fortunate that he got what he wanted and more from two of his three employees. In most situations I have come across, companies and the executives who run them are not so lucky. When a leader hands over or authorizes resources, along with that transfer he must communicate three things: the value and importance of the task at hand; confidence in the subordinate's ability to succeed; and the expectation of a positive outcome. The manager must also convey the hope that the employee or subordinate will take ownership of the project. These can be subtle messages, especially if the employee or subordinate isn't used to working in a collaborative adult work environment, or if she has worked in toxic work environments in the past. So, you should not convey resources with a lecture that says, "Okay, pretty boy, you had better produce..." Instead, the manager should express that he sees something in an employee or subordinate; the manager should verbalize that he recognizes the employee's or subordinate's talents and skills; that the employee's or subordinate's potential is clear, that he wants to see it actualized, and here are the tools to make it happen. Sound like a workplace scenario that would inspire you? It would—and has—inspired me, and I've seen this approach inspire many others as well.

In the previous chapter, on leadership, the difference I highlighted between leadership and management was that the leader has to be a resource. But the leader must walk a fine line. I have seen many situations where the leader has offered herself as a resource, only to find the employees and subordinates misperceive that generosity. They think the leader is an equal member of the team, with equal onus to do the work. But that's not the leader's job, and it would cramp her ability to lead if she focused so closely on just one project; it would bring about a myopia. Instead the leader should say, "I'm here. But don't lean on me. If, however, there is a question about direction or alignment, about meeting objectives, I won't do your work, but I will be a sounding board and a beacon, so your course is never in doubt."

Here's a real-world example that blends a number of the points I have made in this chapter into a good illustration of what I am driving at. One of the companies that I consult with is Minitab. I mentioned the company earlier in this book, and I cite it again here because I think it is an exemplary company. Minitab produces statistical analysis software, and it is focused on quality assurance and Six Sigma protocols. Minitab has solid, active competitors, but Minitab dominates the market. So, although Minitab pays close attention to the competition, the immediate risk of a competitive threat isn't foremost in their minds.

Recently, Minitab's chief executive officer, Barbara Ryan, decided that the company had an opportunity to provide its clients with better opportunities to be successful using Minitab software. She and her technical team got together and started to map out a path to reconfigure how Minitab takes new software features from concept to general availability. But further analysis showed that it would take an investment and an effort to totally restructure how the various Minitab teams moved through the software development processes. They all realized the process had to move from a classical model to an agile platform. However, to do this, Minitab had to change not only the critical path for software development, but also the perspective of the people who would do the work. Barbara Ryan made the decision to move ahead and invest in the training, hardware, and software for the agile platform. But change has to be communicated to the developers, and she couldn't just go in there, bark out a few *like-it-or-lump-it* orders to indicate that the classical approach was out and the agile platform was in, and... "If you are not on board with the change, we'll go out and find someone who is."

Instead, Ryan addressed the software teams and said, "We want to do things differently. You are the people who will make this happen, and we will give you every possible tool and resource you require to get to the new platform." She also communicated her genuine excitement about the project. Why? Because the new platform would enable Minitab to deliver new software releases and updates months earlier than was possible using the old design methodology, the classical platform. It was a move that was great for the customers, great for the company, but, moreover, it was also great for the developers, because the developers were learning as they contributed—they were growing, becoming better, wiser, more skilled...for themselves and for Minitab—win-win-win! They might experience some pain along the way during the transition, but they ultimately would share an investment they would own for their entire careers.

Candidly, Ryan and every Minitab leader knew that the organization was taking a risk by introducing the teams to highly portable and highly marketable skills. After all, workers are volunteers, not indentured servants. But Minitab would also be remembered by these programmers as a company that granted them autonomy, resources, power, and control; a company that allowed them to take ownership of the project, that promoted career and personal growth. The result was renewed dedication to the outcome desired by the company, and a genuine alignment between personal goals and organizational goals. As a result, the respect of the organization for the staff and of the staff was clearly visible, and each took ownership for the achievement of Minitab's goals. Voluntary turnover, which was never a threat, has reached an all-time low, and intracompany cooperation and camaraderie is at a new high and pleasing (to all). Plus, every one of these Tabbers, as the Minitab employees call themselves, knows and feels the glow of being a respected link in a chain of current and future success. The employees at Minitab are at home, and few competitors could lure them from a company that makes it clear to them every day that they matter and that they make a difference.

But giving autonomy and providing resources cannot independently carve out a formula for success. Leaders must **guide** and participate, nurture and **guide**, act as a **guiding** beacon.

Let me close by telling you the story of a dot-com that I worked for a few years back. It was a company named BuildNet (I say "was" because it's not around any more). With its solid vision of optimizing the building materials supply chain, BuildNet raised $147,000,000 in venture capital. (Yes, that's one hundred forty-seven million dollars—at that time the largest single venture investment in the Southeast.) There were immediate prospects for a successful **initial public offering (IPO)**. So, in 1999 and 2000, BuildNet was able to lure top talent at every level of the company: leaders, managers, employees—you name it. No expense was spared, and BuildNet was described in the local press as having established a dream team of leaders and managers. I was attracted to BuildNet after my retirement from SAS Institute by the prospect of enough resources, autonomy, and power to create an *employer-of-choice environment* in a technology startup. By late 2001, BuildNet had burned through its $147 million, hired and subsequently laid off 1,200 employees, and collapsed in bankruptcy with an additional $100,000,000 (yes, that's one hundred million dollars) in debt, to say nothing of the lawsuits stacking up like planes trying to land at LaGuardia on Christmas Eve.

What happened?

Well, BuildNet had the talent (with a history of remarkable leadership and accomplishments), ample resources, and vision. But it lacked two crucial elements: Standards of Performance (accountability) and the compelling need to deliver results.

BuildNet had great vision and that vision attracted talent and resources. Had BuildNet achieved a balance between leadership and accountability, had it insisted on a culture where employees took ownership of projects and where leaders articulated expectations and reviewed progress and results, things might have turned out differently. There might have been a successful BuildNet IPO. Instead BuildNet will go down as one of the Dot-Com Bubble Busters.

So you see it's not just money and budgets, or vision and dream teams. It's a blend of all those things—great people, a great culture, and accountability to the customer and to the bottom line.

5

Demand Contribution; Be Worthy of Receiving It

There's a big difference between making an effort, even a heroic effort, and making a contribution. Yet even though they are different—and offer wildly different outcomes—the vast majority of organizations, executives, and managers regularly demand the wrong one. Instead of requiring *contribution from the people they hire and pay*, they opt for demanding *effort, and the visible evidence of same*, whether it be face time, volume of output, maximum activity, or even the healthy glow of perspiration. The problems for organizations arise because managers who focus on effort are likely to 1) characterize "high energy," perpetual motion employees as "A" players, and 2) view those special talents who appear to breeze through projects and processes without much stress or wasted motion as uncommitted, or worse.

Managers who demand effort instead of contribution are seeing the workplace much like a nonhomemaker (me, for example) sees the automatic washing machine in the family laundry. The machine whirrs, spins, and sloshes the clothes around, and there is much agitation. So the uninitiated person (me, again) assumes that outstanding results, immaculately clean clothes, are forthcoming. And that's a desirable and greatly productive outcome. However, there are washing machines, and there are washing machines.

When leaders approach the parts they play in accomplishing tasks through people, and their manager-employee relations, in this same way they really expose two organizational vulnerabilities, both damaging to the process of building an engaged workforce: They reveal their naiveté of how to build long-term sustainable value through people; and they wrongly communicate what the organization values are. If an organization repeatedly signals that it demands and rewards effort, it is only a matter of time before it gets what it asks for: a lot of motion without a focus on results. That's bad enough, but worse is the probability that the employees who have a bias and a commitment to producing positive outcomes, see that productivity is not the key to personal success and migrate to "the dark side." And why not? It is certainly easier to run in place than it is to cover any ground—uphill, downhill, and into the wind.

Once the "reward for effort" mode is established it is a short decline into an accelerating cycle of cynicism and disingenuous behavior where even the best and the brightest of your employees add to the problems. Employees say to themselves, and sometimes to others, "There is little difference in the recognition given to me when I deliver results, and to Joe or Mary when they put in extra hours or face time without results. So, I guess just showing up **is** 75 percent of the game. Why should I do more, accomplish more, care more, if the bosses don't? It doesn't make sense for me to care more than the execs. After all it's their company!"

Game over! The toxicity has set in. Your best and brightest see no logical alignment between achievement, commitment, and engagement.

Well, I think you get the picture.

Now the question is, are you aware of the way your own reward system is working? Does it discriminate between effort and contribution? Let's take a look through a somewhat unique example. A few years ago I worked for a short time for a fairly large Business-to-Business dot-com, where I was brought in to put the pieces in place to fashion this company into an *employer of choice*. Though the arc of that company's short history can be expressed in just eight words (greed, arrogance, impatience, naiveté, spending, debt, burnout, and bankruptcy), we did have some very talented management staff. One guy who landed there before I arrived was a capable, but inexperienced, director of corporate communications. He was a smart young man, with great feel and skill for the job, and he had real passion for his work. But as the dot-com grew to employ more than 1,200 employees, it was clear to me that he was in deep water when it came to picking up on the signals that were flashing brightly in that environment.

What fascinated me about him was that—unlike just about everyone else I encountered there—he didn't seem to be in it for the money, or the stock options, and the potentially lucrative initial public stock offering (IPO). He was involved in the work and displayed a commitment to getting results. He was effective as all get-out. He got us press coverage on a global scale, and he built solid relationships with the analyst community. But he was frustrated all the time. His angst came from the fact that the dot-com world he had entered revealed itself to be largely made up of motion, smoke, and mirrors, with little interest in outcomes and deliverables. (Remember the "dot-bomb Year 2000? We could have been the Poster Children.) You see, although he had a frantic energy about him, and he always looked to me as though he was rushing to a three-alarm fire, he did his best work out of the sight and hearing range of the high-flyers on the executive staff.

I pulled him aside one day, sat him down in a rare calm moment, and asked, "Why do you always skip around here as though your hair is on fire?" He answered that his perception was that this was a dot-com and what dot-coms really valued was *fast forward motion* [read *effort*]. He said he knew that if he didn't look as though he were manically tumbling forth, the results he produced, and, therefore he, wouldn't be valued—his career would suffer.

A classic case. Textbook. This guy was committed and capable of adding mountains of value to the company. But he didn't see results as the notable factor of his presence; he was led to believe that his *effort, and its appearance,* was the really valuable commodity. He didn't see that the results of his work were his mark on the company because he was led to believe otherwise.

When I asked him why he had that impression, why he had to look and act frantic to give the impression he was adding value, he said he had observed who the "players" were within the company and who got praised and/or listened to. He saw that little attention was paid to outcome, and lots of fanfare was heaped on activity and motion. Although no one had told him that effort was the valuable commodity, he could see the reality clearly, and figured it was the path to riches, both tangible and psychological. It took awhile, and some interesting run-ins between him and a few of the gasbags around the office, to convince him otherwise.

There is a moral to this parable, and it applies far beyond dot-coms. *Don't demand effort; demand contribution.* And the only way to effectively demand contribution is to show employees where their contribution adds to the big picture, where an employee's contribution adds to the organization's overall goals.

Too simple a moral to be applicable or true? Is this common knowledge a little too common?

Come on, let's face it, if you ask the average employees of a Fortune 1000 company how they add value or how what they do adds value to the organization *today*, *right now*, what do you think most of them would say? I know the answer. You do too, I suspect. Most of them don't have a clue. Oh, they would be able to tell you *what* they do—in terms of daily tasks and routines. And they'd be able to tell you what they think they are *paid to do*. Some may even venture to say that they are a gear in a large machine that drives the enterprise forward. But the overwhelming majority of them have no idea what and how they contribute to the fortunes of the company that employs them. Typically, no one has ever told them, or better yet, showed them how what they do is not just an effort, but a contribution to a win-win-win paradigm: a personal win in terms of their professional development and ability to continue to earn a good living; the enhancement of the company's bottom line, brand, and reputation; and the value delivered to the customer by the company's products and/or services.

Now, let me give you some very clear examples of what I am talking about. One is an abstract example that you can apply today, and the other is one you'll probably never see in your lifetime.

You may employ an office receptionist, a person to answer phones, sort mail, greet visitors, and control access, right? Okay, take a piece of paper and write down the person's job description. Include a primary duty or two and limit yourself to two or three sentences. Piece of cake, right? Are you sure?

My bet would be that most of you wrote some variation of the following: answers phones and greets visitors in the waiting room, sorts mail and keeps the reception room looking neat and clean.

Well, that may accurately describe the regular activity and the *effort* the person must exert. And maybe that's what was advertised in the job posting or newspaper. **Help Wanted**: *Person to answer phones and greet visitors....*

Do such ads and postings attract candidates who have the interest and potential to make a meaningful contribution and who are willing to be value producers? My guess is that the people who respond are more likely to be those who seek a paycheck and benefits, not those who want to help your company become a competitive force. You see, the posting is focused on the effort expected, the routine. And frankly, the job sounds boring, when described in terms of effort and duties.

But what if you were to describe the job in terms of its significance and *contribution potential*? Let me write the want ad for you. **Help Wanted**: *Customer service-oriented individual to act as receptionist and to manage the first contact that visitors, vendors, business partners, guests, and callers have with our company. Must serve simultaneously as ambassador and representative of our image and our brand(s); other clerical duties as assigned.*

I think you might get some better resumes. You will hear from people who want to be part of something larger, people who want to satisfy one of the most basic human needs: to belong, to count, to contribute—to add value.

Here's another example. Recently, I was asked to do some work with the CIA. (Yes *that* CIA.) It was a fascinating engagement because the CIA, like any large organization that strives to be great, is concerned with attracting and retaining top-grade people. But that part of the CIA's efforts is for another part of this book. Right now, I want to talk about the "seal."

When you enter CIA Headquarters, the main building, you walk by, or over, the impressive CIA seal. And man, it is impressive! It lays imbedded in the floor of the main reception area; it is spotless, spit-shined, and who knows what else they do to it. Every time I have seen it, it looks the same: shining, pristine, immaculate, daunting, and impressive.

If the custodian who maintains the reception hall, saw his role as nothing more than keeping the floor clean, I doubt that I and others would be as impressed with the area. But what I learned in casual conversations with CIA employees is that it is made clear to the maintenance crews at the agency that part of the value they bring is in keeping the appearance of the facility worthy and representative of the status and mission of the agency.

Do you think that the custodian who maintains the spotless condition of that seal takes pride is his job? You bet he does. It's obvious. Do you think that the janitor is focused on *effort*? Or on *contribution*? I am guessing that janitor is focused on contribution. He clearly knows what part, if small, his work activities play in the overall impression that the CIA wishes to convey to visitors. I am sure it was communicated to him during the hiring process. Even though the placement ad probably described this job as "custodian for a large government agency." The value of the position was likely described as "diligent, dutiful worker needed to contribute to maintaining the image of the world's most prominent and notable intelligence-gathering organization."

Let me ask you this: Are you advertising for and hiring "janitors for a large company"? Or are you recruiting "diligent, dutiful workers needed to contribute to maintaining the image of one of America's most-admired companies"? And can you guess the cost to your company, to your brand, to your customer experience, *and* to your bottom line by having a broom pusher in that role, instead of someone who recognizes the role they play in "shining the seal," so to speak?

Now let's move this concept up the chain of command, and to your organization. Migrate the discussion from the level of janitors and receptionists, as important as they are. Let's look at employees in IT, sales support, HR, marketing, tech support, engineering, and manufacturing. Think about the staff in accounting, and the middle managers, regional managers, project managers, and even senior management. Speaking metaphorically: Do they behave as solitary workers—answering phones, pushing brooms, and exerting disconnected effort? Or do they view themselves, their work, and their results as contributors to the mission of the company? Do they behave as first responders to the needs of customers and fellow employees? Do they see where they fit and the impact of their work on the big picture?

Motivating For and Evaluating Employee Contribution

It's a given that great organizations have carefully nurtured cultures. But that is only part of the battle to draw the best possible contribution from employees. That culture has to be wisely and regularly communicated, so the employees know and recognize without doubt what part they play in the company's progress and ultimately in the customer experience. They must be advised regarding what a contribution means and what it looks like. And they must be told that contribution is what is expected, what counts, and what will be counted.

For example, the IT staff must know and understand that when they keep the Internet up and all the databases fully accessible, the *customer will be the eventual winner through* a better experience, which keeps them loyal, which keeps the company profitable and growing. The marketing communications teams must see the part collateral material plays in the presentation of the company to customers and prospects, and how much even a typo in a brochure could damage the brand, "scuff the seal," so to speak. The same is true for the sales support, because their contribution is part of something larger, the total sales effort and the ways the customer experience is set in motion by sales reps and account managers. This is true for every department, for every member of your organization. And only the executive team, the leadership, can authentically communicate the connection between each employee and the bottom line.

The message must be "You are important; what you do is important; the result of your effort is important; you can add value; we expect you to add value; and recognition, reward, and advancement will be based on your ownership and response to those challenges."

So you see, it's not how many autos roll off an assembly line and are shipped out on car carriers that count. It's the employees' connection to the impact their work has on customers and prospects that brings the recognition of contribution full circle. Ultimately it's the organization's obligation to communicate that impact to everyone who contributes.

Now it may seem to you and me that the *effort* of installing power steering units on new minivans would be a boring task. But is it a stretch for us to imagine the value to the company to have assembly line workers recognizing the importance of their role in the driving experience of the vehicles' future owners, the possibility that they are a part of driver comfort, owner satisfaction, and even future sales? Doesn't it help employees' commitment to producing great results to also know that an owner's experience and satisfaction may mean stable employment and a better financial future for them and their peers? That's the kind of employee communication and message that elevates efforts to contribution.

What are the metrics for determining contribution? They can't be the same for everyone. Not everyone can contribute at the same level. And not everyone should be expected to contribute at the same level. An organization that values only superstars and A players won't have the support staff essential to keep those A players on point. And those lesser, but essential, contributions need to be recognized. The salesman who puts up seven figure numbers each year—the equivalent of a high scoring forward on a championship basketball team—couldn't even be on the court, per se, without the passes (opportunities) vetted by sales support, and the plays (strategies) coordinated by marketing, or the coaching (team leadership) from management that put that salesman in position to score.

So, the measurement of various types of contribution is essential, and one way to evaluate it is how the individuals—superstars, to B team, to reserves—materially contribute to the organization's goals. The actual metrics vary from sector to sector. It may be sales contracts signed, or customer satisfaction metrics, product innovations, patents filed, Web site visits, cars sold, tables waited on, units shipped, cases won, or accounts renewed. The list of possibilities is endless, but must be specific to your organization.

When determining rewards, note that—as I point out elsewhere in this book—reward is not always and foremost about money. Money is important, there's no doubt, and paying competitively fair wages is essential to keeping good workers (it's one expression of how much you value their contribution!), but you should not be surprised to see how much *recognition of contribution through encouraging word or open praise or noted appreciation* is important to your employees, and how many would freely chuck a job where they were paid well but treated with ennui.

So, *how* you express that sense of an employees' value may well be as important as *what's* expressed. If you treat (or seem to treat) workers like indentured servants who have no options, or treat them like interchangeable parts, or if you are disingenuous in your praise, employees quickly learn that they aren't really important and, perhaps worse, that you're not being truthful. They will say, "Why should I do more, when it's clear that you don't think I am important?" That thought is often followed by something like: "You don't really care about me, so I won't care about what is important to you—product, customer, or bottom line."

Here's one approach you might consider. It's low cost, and very effective. Another company I have worked with is American Eagle Outfitters (AEO). I admire the way they work to instill their associates with the pride of being part of the American Eagle team. And one of the ways they do this is simply by asking them what they think. I know that seems too simple to be a solution for a complex problem, but it's not. The executive leadership of the company travels around the country encouraging in-person feedback from their associates, even part-time associates. And they welcome comments on everything from the presentation of current product offerings to what goods should be developed for retail sales. That one act graphically demonstrates to these associates that they are important, that American Eagle cares about what you say, and about what you think, so you must be of worth, of value—important. It says that these associates are part of the team that includes everyone, from the highest levels of our leadership to the part-time sales associate.

Let me close out this chapter by talking about another company, DePuy Orthopedics, a Johnson & Johnson company. Their business is manufacturing, marketing, and selling replacement shoulders, knees, and hips. They make the actual devices. What's unique about DePuy is that they are focused on maintaining a high level of interest in their products among their sales force, yet their sales force is largely made up of independent contractors. The leadership of DePuy came to me to ask how to develop sales leaders who can get people who were not employees to remain engaged and to understand how they contribute to the overall success of themselves, DePuy, client, and patient.

Now typically with an independent sales force, you don't really control their effort the way you might be able to among an employed sales base. (Frankly, even if you could control them, I doubt it would result in a positive outcome, because outcomes are not about control.) What you hope is to influence them to be motivated in line with the company's mission and values.

Here's the simple solution: Introduce each of the members of the sales team to the company's win-win-win philosophy via early contact with a person who has successfully used a DePuy product—a surgeon, or preferably a patient. You want them to push the rock up the hill, day in and day out? You want them to work hard, with laser focus? Why not have them interact with the people they've helped through their work? Or the injured people they *might* help with their sales efforts.

You talk about a triple win! The sales force would not only feel great and make more money, but the company would win by having such a passionate sales force on the street—boosting its brand, customer loyalty, and bottom line—and the patients (customers) will have the highest-quality goods available to them; their lives will improve as a result of DePuy.

Simply put, the sales force has to recognize and appreciate what part they play in that patient's success/that surgeon's success. By seeing a successful outcome and the role they have played (or can play) in allowing people to, say, walk again, that will affect even their tone of voice when making sales calls. It will affect the way they dress, and how aggressively and passionately they develop relationships with doctors and hospitals. Why? They are not road warriors selling a mechanical device; they are purveyors of healing; they are helping people; they touch people's lives.

Note that this sales force can't generate this passion and this sense of contribution on its own. It has to be shrewdly and authentically done by the organization's leadership, and that leadership has to have a clear vision of the difference between effort and contribution. Then, without being disingenuous, the leadership has to be prepared to leverage this sense of contribution for the benefit of all involved.

6

Applaud Effort; Reward Contribution

Nearly every person who comes to work for you wants to contribute in some way; they want to do something worthwhile, something worthy of their talents. But we all know that A-tier, B-tier, and C-tier performers are often playing on the same court. So, it's crucial that you establish a reward system that is commensurate with the contributions made and expected from team members. The ways that rewards, tangible and intangible, are aligned with the significance and magnitude of results plays a major role in making behavior modeling and behavior modification work for your engaged workplace architecture. You see, if we go back again to Maslow and his hierarchy of human needs, people are looking for recognition for what they accomplish. They are quick to recognize which behaviors/outcomes are rewarded. And, if they have the skills and aptitude, they are quick to adapt to find ways to earn the ego strokes. No secret sauce, no smoke and mirrors.

There is an old story about President Abraham Lincoln's leadership skill that, whether accurate or myth, lends itself to this "rule" for building an engaged workforce. The situation is said to have happened in the middle years of the American Civil War. (We in the South more commonly refer to it as "The War Between the States," and some, less diplomatically, as "The War of Northern Aggression.") It is told that while many of the Union generals gave maximum effort in their pursuit of the war, Ulysses Grant was the most strategically, tactically, and militarily successful of the Union generals. While other

Union commanders were both loyal and hard-working, none were producing Grant-like results. However, Grant had a tendency to drink on the job.

Under pressure from the military high command, moralistic politicians, and "do-gooders" to deal with Grant's "personal issues," Lincoln made his point by directing one of his aides to learn which brand of liquor was Grant's drink of choice, and to send a case of it to each of the other generals. Produce results; earn rewards. Reward contribution, not effort!

People have a core need to be recognized, and when an organization recognizes an individual, it acknowledges that this individual and the organization are in sync—that the person is valuable, notable, and worthy. This not only provides immediate fulfillment for a core human need, but it also is essential for initiating and sustaining the cycle of engaging employees.

However, it is important to understand that you *can* initiate and sustain an engagement environment based on rewarding effort rather than contribution. But if you do so, the incentives for your employees to be "productive" wane, and you cultivate a workforce focused on looking good rather than doing good.

So it comes down to this: Yes, expect genuine effort and hard work, but reward getting something done, and having that something be of value to your mission to build competitive advantage.

In a previous chapter, I talked about demanding contribution instead of effort, and I pointed out the importance of being worthy of extraordinary contribution by valuing it properly. I also pointed out the central role of communicating to employees what role they play in the overall company plan, to the point of introducing them to the customers whose lives they have affected (hopefully in a positive way).

It's clear to me that it's of paramount importance to applaud the efforts of employees. At the same time, you need to reserve rewards for real accomplishments that bring about positive outcomes. So, let's look a little closer at this, because it is a central point to engaging employees.

Let's consider, for example, a top-level individual contributor, and let's say you pay him a base salary of $150,000. Now he's a high wage earner, in the top five percent of the nation for salary. But are you paying that salary for his effort? My guess is that it's assumed he will give extraordinary effort—you are paying for the results. But how do you structure the reward system so you *applaud* his effort but *reward* his contribution? Candidly the "applause," per se, for his efforts is inherent in the fact that you employ him, that he has a key role in the strategic plan of the organization, and that his salary reflects all of that. So, the salary is there in recognition of potential, aptitude, and the expectation of results, of contribution. To show how to structure a reward system for him and people throughout your company, let's look at a sports analogy.

Think about major league baseball. Take a first-year player. Not a superstar but a promising prospect. He signs a contract for a six-figure salary so the team can lock him up, observe him, and see how he contributes. He becomes a part of the regular lineup.

Okay, let's say at the end of the year he has produced a batting average of .230, with 40 RBIs, and 3 HRs. (For those of you who are not baseball fans, this is slightly below average. An average batter contributes one out of every four times he is at bat.) Let's say further he has committed 15 errors, and his on-base percentage was less than 25 percent, or .250. (That's bad performance.) But he plays hard. He runs out every hit, his uniform is filthy because he's not afraid of the hard slide, and he's always cheering his teammates on—a great clubhouse influence, as they say. At the end of the year, he says he really believes he has earned a raise because he has worked so hard.

You are the general manager. What is your response? The correct response should be that the management applauds the effort but can't reward him because his production was low. To keep him interested, he might get some small cost-of-living adjustment, and A-for-effort. But it would be irresponsible and possibly damaging to the rest of the team, to the real contributors, if he were rewarded disproportionately to the numbers he really put up that year.

So, an employee can be a B player and be paid a just salary to "put up okay numbers—batting .230," working hard every day to get the job done efficiently, and still be of value. He's worth his pay if he gets the job done in time, without error, and elevates the team with his spirit. He's got a role. He plays it very well, even though he'll never be top dog.

That said, it's just as important to recognize that there are people in an organization for whom there are lower expectations. After all, it's unrealistic to expect everyone in the organization to be a superstar, and these types of journeyman players—essential to a team in their own way—shouldn't be discounted just because they don't "put up big numbers" every year. However, the rewards given to them should be in accordance with the organization's expectations and given with the understanding that while not everyone is expected to contribute at the same level, some contribution is required to have a role at all.

When doing so, keep in mind why people work, and what an earlier chapter revealed about work and its role in the "belonging" of all of us, and ask yourself: Why do they choose to work for me? Why do they come back in the morning, again and again, when they really don't have to, when they have other options? In good work settings, it's because the organization gives them interesting work to do and because they see or feel that the organization gives them the opportunity to learn and grow. They also like to be around other good people, since the workplace has become the nexus for our social interactions, a place where the employee's surrogate "family" meets every day. As the "business family" gathers each day, it's really a parallel family environment.

It is also important for leaders to recognize that sometimes, hopefully not often, companies and executives hire the wrong people. These are employees who are disinterested, or even disruptive—players who don't fit. Indeed, some employees clearly exert no effort and really are just placeholders. They may bring skill, talent, work history, and a track record to the team, but they don't want to play. In some cases, they are better than having nobody in the role, but not by much. Leaders must always being looking to "trade up" for that position to get an A or solid B player, but it's clear that these people should be managed out, and as quickly as possible. By the way, my experience has shown me that: 1) they are recognized early on by their peers and subordinates; 2) they have self awareness; and, 3) management is typically last to identify them.

To underscore a point I made in a previous chapter, let me tell you about when I worked at Liggett Group, Inc., in the late 1970s. At that time, Liggett Group was the parent of Liggett & Myers Tobacco Company. While there, I worked along the same hallway with a guy we'll call Sal. Everyone who worked in the office marveled at Sal because at the close of every day he would pack two large briefcases full with notes and papers before heading home. No one knew what was really in there, but they were heavy, and Sal—who did not appear to be physically fit—would strain under the effort to lug those over-laden bags out to his car. (The office joke was that he was selling his neighbors reams of paper out of the supply closet.) Yet, in the course of work each day, it was very clear to even the most casual observer that nothing productive was coming from Sal's desk. There was no positive outcome to the apparent effort. Nothing was actually getting done. I am sure if you asked him if he was a contributor, he would look surprised and say, "Can't you see all the stuff I am working on? I take work home every night for goodness sakes!" There may have even been a high level of emotional investment from Sal in getting things done; goodness knows he seemed to try. But Sal confused effort with contribution, and he really did nothing to "move the rock up the hill."

Another thing that was clear about Sal and how he was viewed by the company: No one at Liggett had communicated to him what he was supposed to contribute. No one told him that if he just exerted himself with no outcome, he wasn't really doing anyone any good.

The management at the time may not have recognized the difference themselves, and Sal hung on there, convinced he was moving mountains, where he was more than likely creating roadblocks, and unwittingly so. Sal got small raises and interim promotions, just like everyone else—because at that time, Liggett rewarded effort and never took the time to examine what the effort contributed to in terms of outcome. Who knows, Sal may still be there or at some other large bureaucracy, lugging those overstuffed bags home every night.

Frankly, it's toxic to reward effort. Why? Well, if you start to reward effort, the people who are making real contributions—and believe me, they know who they are *and* they know each other—will see their efforts as denigrated. I know that we felt that way at Liggett about Sal. If you are rewarding the churners—the ones who are just putting in the time, packing the briefcase with work to take home each night but never really getting anything done—at the same or a similar level to that which you are rewarding the people who are propelling the organization forward, you are tearing down your company's will to be productive. The contributors will see that rewards are tied to the wrong metrics and that the company is indeed rewarding motion not results. And since getting results is a big and long-term commitment, the best and brightest will respond to the established reward system, and productivity will stall and backslide. Management will be no more the wiser, either, because they continue to focus on evidence of effort.

Back to the baseball diamond, if you don't mind. If you reward the .230 hitter with the history of errors and low on-base percentage in any way similarly to the perennial all-star who hits .340, compiles 110 RBIs, and swats 40 home runs, just on the basis of all-out effort, a dirty uniform, and clubhouse camaraderie, what's the incentive for the all-star to work on his game, keep in shape, and continue to produce at the plate and in the field?

Managing Out the Nonperformers

Not many of us want to return to the days of Dickens and corporal punishment at the workplace (though I have been tempted now and then to welcome it with open arms!), so you have to figure out another way to punish those who are not contributors. Maybe "punish" is too strong a word. Maybe we take this in an end-around way, because there is really no need for punishment. No need for sanctions. If someone isn't doing his job and isn't even a third-tier player (meaning he is not only unable to push the rock up the hill but actively dragging it down into the valley), you have to get rid of him. That person must be managed out. This is how it was once at GE under Jack Welsh, when he managed out 10 percent of his workforce *each year*, while rewarding just the top 20 percent of his performers with stocks and bonuses.

To manage out the nonperformers, you have to create a model for evaluating their contribution, and that model has to be based on that person's capability—not just on some abstract ideal of performance that is universally and unilaterally applied to everyone in the company. (Remember, we can't all be quarterbacks.) Once you have established that model and communicated it clearly to the employees, the choice of whether a bad employee stays or goes is really up to them, in the end. They will be able to clearly see where they are not measuring up. With metrics in place, you not only have the chance to cull out the people who are not propelling the organization to competitive advantage, but you have guidelines for hiring replacements whose interests, spirit, and capabilities are in alignment with your organization's goals. With that new hire, you can focus that employee's energy on creating a tangible and highly desirable outcome.

So, with an approach like this, you never have to rely on punishing people. Besides, punishing people isn't a very good use of time and energy, and it usually focuses on revenge, not a sincere effort to motivate a deadbeat employee. If someone isn't capable of focusing on outcomes, because of lack of skill, personality, or intellect, there's little you can do with that person anyway, since she is unmanageable. There's little that can motivate her except the powerful force of withholding recognition and rewards.

I agree that the withholding of recognition and reward is a passive methodology. But there is a universal desire for people to be recognized and rewarded. Yes, even people who exert no effort want recognition and rewards, and if they are not getting it at work, and unable to change their behavior to earn it, it won't be long before they will go to some other place of work to find it—perhaps to the enduring benefit of your organization.

How to determine rewards? Today's reward structures are flat, and they should be curved. Here's why. First, let's recognize the obvious. Big contributors need big rewards, but keep in mind what I pointed out in an earlier chapter: Not everyone can contribute at the highest level, and rewards have to reflect that. I am not saying that the marketing copywriter should be rewarded for a good slogan at the same rate as the top salesman. But the reward should be something meaningful to that low-level marketing copywriter in terms of the salary he makes. More importantly, when rewarding people in the *same* job tier and category (or nearly the same tier and category), you have to be careful to make the rewards truly meaningful to your people. Adding to the challenge, you have to use your reward structure as a way of signaling to B players with good potential that they are not yet the top bananas, but were they to be so, you pay bananas very well.

Let's take an example. In a flat reward system, the top people get healthy bonuses, and the noncontributors get nothing. Unfortunately, the spread between the top tiers of performers may be as flat as to act as a disincentive at bonus time. If I were to say that the top salesperson gets a ten percent bonus for selling $2,000,000 per year, and the guy who sells nothing gets zero bonus, you'd think that was a fair reward system, right?

The top guy has been knocking it out of the park, and if his base is $250,000, he's getting $25,000. Thing is, there are other sales guys with nearly that same base who are selling just $1,000,000 per year. With a flat bonus structure, they are not getting a five percent bonus, or half what the top guy gets. They may get an eight percent or nine percent bonus, to keep a respectful distance from the bottom. At this rate, the sales guys with good base salaries who are coasting and selling next to nothing would be getting at least a cost-of-living increase and then some each year—for no effort and no contribution.

Now does that ten percent bonus seem fair?

So, under that flat structure, there is little relative reward for being a high-level contributor. To see this clearly, let's go to a sports metaphor again and compare two players: One plays second base and one play shortstop. They both have just finished their rookie years, where they both made $200,000. The second baseman batted .330, had 35 HRs, 112 RBIs, and a fielding percentage of 950. The shortstop batted .240, had 6 HRs, and 45 RBIs, and fielding percentage of 870. In the baseball world, in the second year, the second baseman— a better player—gets $1,000,000, and the shortstop will again make just $200,000 (or maybe a small amount more) his second year, until he improves his contribution.

With $1,000,000 going to his friend the second baseman, the shortstop has a dramatic example of what is in store for him *if* he improves in the next season, because the differential in salary and bonus is truly reflective of the two players' dramatically different levels of contribution.

In the corporate world, you have to take this lesson to heart and provide rewards and recognition that serve as an incentive for everyone to improve and avoid sending a message to your top people that everyone in the organization is "just about equal in the end."

Finally, another aspect of reward systems to keep in mind is that the workplace is in many ways a familylike social structure. (In another chapter I explain how this has become so, especially in the last 30 years.) Just as in a family, the workplace must applaud effort and reward contribution. As you structure your reward and recognition systems, keep in mind that people like to be around other people who are just like them. And people who are of like minds communicate openly, which you can use to your benefit as a manager. Frankly, this workplace family nexus presents a natural opportunity (a transparent forum, where trusting, like-minded people share ideas and gossip) to see the rewards given for performance and contribution. Given the choice, I know for a fact that coworkers would rather associate with winners than losers. They would rather align their professional fates with winners rather than losers. So, at the workplace, like-minded people, both ambitious and successful, are comingling and learning from each other. When one fellow says, "I hear Johnny's put up the big numbers this quarter" everyone smiles. He's on top. But everyone also sees how Johnnie is meaningfully rewarded. And everyone of like mind naturally wants to be like Johnny, to win and reap those same rewards. To your benefit, you as a manager have planted the seeds for a workplace camaraderie that will be the envy of every other manager who seeks to build a high-productivity environment where excellence thrives and naturally propagates itself.

7

Cheerlead; The "Magic" of M&Ms

Any successful executive must accomplish several tasks. He must pick the right people, give guidance, describe expectations, and provide resources to allow employees to grow. A savvy executive should clear pathways and remove impediments to employees' success and, yes, even cheerlead.

Like, *rah-rah* cheerlead? *Yes.* As embarrassing and potentially undignified as that initially sounds, leaders and managers should stand on the sidelines and say and do something heartfelt, meaningful, and encouraging for their employees and team members. And they should do so with authentic spiritedness. Let the employees know that their actions are in alignment with the organization's vision; that they are making progress, keeping up, or falling behind; and that what they are straining to do is in sync with the organization's goals.

What's so important about that? Well, an engaged workforce needs cheerleaders. Or let me say it another way: You can't have an engaged workforce without cheerleading. It's not childish or belittling to let the employees know that they are doing a good job. As stony-faced and tough as some of your employees may seem, you'd be surprised how much they crave a little encouragement and how that encouragement readily translates to redoubled commitment, which produces better and quicker high-quality results. In fact, nothing makes an employee want to do more than to be cheered on and recognized for good work along the way.

Southwest Airlines is all about boosting employee morale, and in the cheerleading department, they have no rivals that I know of. Before I get into specifics, let me ask you: What's your impression of Southwest Airlines? Do you think that it is a happy and profitable company? *Yes.* A fun place to work? *You bet.* A "place of work" where flying around the country day in and day out, dealing with the largely disenchanted traveling public, handing out peanuts and Dr. Pepper doesn't seem like drudgery to the employees? *Yes again.* In fact, Southwest Airlines is renowned for its upbeat, engaged employees, more than it is for its financial success that mocks the industry trends, and its aggression when it challenges competitors where they share routes. And did you know that Southwest is largely unionized?

Remarkably, the cheerleading at Southwest is not reserved for a top-down approach. On the day before Thanksgiving in 2007, my bride of 32 years and I left our home in Durham, North Carolina, for a trip to Nevada. For transportation, we chose Southwest Airlines, more for the convenience of a nonstop flight, than for price, or the stellar reputation of the carrier. We were fortunate to be among the first group of boarders. To my reaffirming pleasure and to my wife's gleeful amusement that morning, each of the Boeing 737's overhead bins had a hand-crafted paper heart taped to it (it's worth noting that Southwest planes have painted hearts on fuselages and tails.) that was imprinted with various sentiments of employee thanks—such as, "We are thankful for our customers"; "We are thankful for our jobs"; "We are thankful for our country"; "We are thankful for our fellow employees"; and even "We are thankful for our company." Cheerleading! I don't know if it was that airplane and that crew on that day. But this I do know: It was spontaneous. I subsequently asked a Southwest official if what we had experienced was scripted from the PR desks in Dallas or dictated from on high. Her response was refreshing; she knew nothing about it, but she was tickled that a Southwest crew or crews thought of it. It's a work environment that cheerleads for the organization's success, for the department's success, for the

individual's success, and for the successful relationships with customers, vendors, and all comers. And it's that enthusiasm, that
engagement with the job, the company, the service they bring, and
with each other that each employee takes to her next task. Oh, and its
ticker symbol on the New York Stock Exchange is LUV. No kidding.
(Remember, Southwest's are the airplanes in the sky with a big heart
painted on the side.) No surprise then that cheerleading is an "engaging" strategy, and it's so much more fun than nit-picking!

Now let's take a step back and take a look at what motivates people, what *genuinely* motivates them. One of the best ways to get people to stretch themselves, to exert the illusive *discretionary effort* is
simply to provide encouragement along the way. As a consultant who
focuses on employee engagement for large and small companies, I am
almost embarrassed to charge my per diem rate only to offer such a
common sense solution to such a pervasive problem. But it's true, and
it really is just that simple. (The challenge is *how* to cheer and encourage and *when* to cheer and encourage, which we deal with later.)

To appreciate the impact of simple encouragement, imagine how
you feel when *your* boss (if he is genuinely aware of what you're
doing) says, *atta boy*. Or *atta girl*. No matter how high you are on the
corporate ladder, it's uplifting. There is no denying it. Sometimes, the
response to encouragement borders on euphoria, a euphoria that
goes far beyond what you're paid or what your bonus is. It's just nice
to be appreciated, to be cheered on. Now, imagine this feeling on a
grander scale, when a team is cheered on. Or a division is cheered on.
Or when the entire company is cheered, applauded, encouraged.
Being genuinely cheered, by an aware CEO or senior executive who
writes or speaks from the heart and not through some PR or polished
corporate messaging, by leaders who are in touch with the task, the
effort, the outcome, and the impact, can actually create an air of
excitement about the challenges and opportunities ahead. When an
organization is encouraged properly, the air of excitement can be sustained over a long period of time, which invariably leads to dramatic

productivity rates, outrageous teamwork, and happy customers. So, when I say that cheerleading is important, it should be a given that the manager or leader has a key role to be *visually enthused* about the person, about the work, about the movement forward, about celebrating milestones.

How does a leader show authentic enthusiasm and not seem patronizing? No matter what industry we are in, whether we are in companies large and small, we all know when a leader is not authentic. That's because most level-headed adults have high sensitivity to hypocrisy, a BS filter. But we are all just as responsive when someone is authentically cheerleading us as individuals because that's what cheerleading is, a genuine affection for the individual, the task, and the outcome. Leaders and managers are making a public acknowledgement that a well-done task is of high value, the outcome has high value, and even the process is of high value. It follows, then, that the individual feels he has high value for having accomplished something so important to the organization's progress.

Back to Southwest Airlines for a moment. An exemplary company like Southwest Airlines celebrates almost every achievement, nearly every milestone. But even Southwest takes care to make sure that the cheerleading and celebrations remain authentic and align with performance against Southwest's values, mission, and goals.

Think of it more like "just-in-time" recognition. If a manager or leader sees something going well, something accomplished, a result delivered, she should cheer it on in public and recognize the employee or group responsible. Encourage and recognize the individual effort that it took to get to here, and enthusiastically applaud that the people and the organization are on the right path. You might have guessed that I would resort to a sports analogy at this point, right? When a soccer player scores a goal, everyone hugs the player who scored the goal. The player who got the assist gets the hugs too. The team is celebrated by the fans. But it's not the championship they've won. Indeed, it's just a milestone in the progress of the game, or the season. Much more is expected of the players, but they receive spot recognition, and they are cheered for where they are at that point in time. Soccer teams don't just celebrate victories; they celebrate the mile markers on the path to victories. And should they lose that particular game, they carry forward the feeling of those small celebrations as an incentive to do even better the next time to achieve more completely. Take the example of the gold-medal winning U.S. Women's Olympic soccer team, the team that had Mia Hamm, Julie Foudy, and Brandi Chastain as players. Those women celebrated *every* goal along their way to the ultimate victory, and with every celebration they lifted each other up. As they did so, they believed they could do more and do better, and that synergy along with the "cheering" of an entire nation (their corporation, if you will), certainly helped propel them to their goal. Well, let's not forget the 2008 women's team as well, where Carli Lloyd scored in the first extra period to give the U.S. a gold medal over Brazil. Hope Solo was one of those getting constant encouragement from her teammates, like Captain Christie Rampone, when she bailed the team out time and again. Remember this! Mia Hamm, the most prolific goal scorer in women's soccer history, was cheered the loudest and longest of her entire career, not for a goal—for an assist!

Refer back to Maslow's hierarchy of needs. The fourth need is "ego stroking," and there's no shame in recognizing that need. Indeed, it's not egotistical to demand a little recognition now and then. When your ego is stroked, you are being sent a message that you are someone important, someone who is valuable. It's also a message that what you do is valuable. And this recognition is tantamount to the recognition of the core worth of the individual.

Most organizations go astray when they think that what people invariably want is more money, benefits, and bonuses. Sure, everyone wants to be paid fairly. There's no doubt about that. But I have learned that pay and benefits are just tangible substitutes for warmth, caring, and recognition of worth. If you set up an organization so that the only way it can express its appreciation for an employee's value is with money, you'll find it's just not enough; it's *never* enough. And it's a never-ending cycle, too; each year you have to one-up yourself with more pay and more trendy benefits, because it's all the "currency" you have with the employee. It's an especially tough position to be in when you exhaust the opportunity for raises, and the employee looks up and says, "What, no raise? You don't like me anymore?"

Unless you genuinely and authentically recognize an employee's value on a person-to-person basis, the warmth and caring will be absent no matter what they are paid. In that case, you should not be surprised when an employee moves on. If you are lucky enough to get a candid exit interview, you may be astonished to hear the employee say, "You never really cared about me or my work," to which you may naively respond: "What, are you joking? We paid you a king's ransom!" In fact, the employee may not have been looking for money. It's actually fairly far down on the list of things that many people want from an organization.

Let's take another example. I have worked with a company in San Antonio called Rack Space. It is a large, Web-hosting company, and they run a tight ship. Every month Rack Space has an open meeting where the CEO, the chairman, and the entire executive team get in front of employees with sleeves rolled up and hair down. All their employees from all over the world are tuned in to the event, called a *Huddle* (sports, again!), and the leadership engages in a cheerleading session. It's not a manic event, and no one breathlessly stomps around the stage. Instead, they tell the employees the status of the business. They explain how they are doing, and what their competitors have been up to. They give a market update, and talk about business performance issues and the solutions required. Then they address the individual departments. They let the department heads explain what has happened recently of major significance and where everyone stands relative to major company objectives. For those of you lucky enough to work in transparent work environments, where financials and accomplishments are shared openly, this may not seem all that extraordinary. But then, at Rack Space, the executive team puts outstanding performers in straitjackets.

Straitjackets? *Yes*.

The mantra for Rack Space is that they provide "fanatical support." So, they put only the most fanatical people, the top customer service performers since the last Huddle, into a straitjacket because they have exhibited that fanaticism; they are living the mission and values of the company. They are just crazy about company performance and customer service.

With this ceremony, the leadership team clearly indicates that these people have performed in great fashion, and it is the highest level of cheerleading. It builds enthusiasm. People at Rack Space are eager to be "jacketed." There is a sense of pride in having worn the jacket, and it helps drive the company employee base to positively fanatical actions that achieve these customer service goals. These employees are well paid to provide service, to perform, with or without the Huddle experience or the jacket, and they all realize that. But this is a fun recognition of an effort as well as of an outcome. It's exemplary of what cheerleading should do to simultaneously reward and motivate an organization.

When I was at SAS Institute, we worked with intensive focus to make it clear to the management that one of their primary jobs was to create a work environment that was compellingly positive. And we offered the management substantial resources to be able to make that happen. The metric of whether we were successful was not how much work we did, or how much money we spent. The metric of the success was the employees' response. If the employees wanted to be in the workplace, we were successful in our obligations as leaders. If the work environment was truly positive, we also noted that the workers—when paid good wages and benefits—didn't focus on wages and benefits as the primary indication of whether they were valued. In the process, we made it part of an ongoing obligation of leadership to stoke the fires of enthusiasm for employees with tangible, visible signs of cheerleading. Nothing hokey or silly. Instead, we encouraged a series of small gestures. It was up to the managers to decide what to do, what was right for their teams. One department manager decided to bring in flowers once a week. Another manager chose to bring in bagels on Friday morning. Now, don't get me wrong. None of the employees thought that the flowers or the bagels were a substitute for raises or bonuses. People aren't stupid, after all. But—and here's the key—these actions *were never meant* to be a substitute for raises and bonuses, and the employees understood that too. Instead they were put in place as a way for the managers to show that they were not there just to supervise. It was to show that the manager had an equal role in expressing how these employees were valued as human beings. It was a way for the managers to express that their employees were worthy of something special. We expressed this companywide as well, with live music, free M&Ms, quality fresh-cooked and baked goods in subsidized café-style eateries, on-site health clinics, low-cost child care, and much more. But those things were *signs* of our concern and genuine affection for our employees, not the sole expression of our concern.

In your organization, if you are not doing this type of cheerleading, you are likely to have cynical employees. Their collective antenna is up, and they may (at least initially) see any efforts to initiate celebrating and cheerleading as being inauthentic stunts. Bring in bagels and flowers, and everyone expects you are going to announce layoffs. It would be as though a woman were in a ho-hum relationship yet suddenly she finds her husband coming home with flowers. It's only natural that she would be expecting bad news. Or at least a request for her husband to go to a bachelor party in Vegas. Accordingly, a cynical relationship between the leadership and the employees is hard to overcome at first. But what if that husband comes home with flowers *every* Friday, for months, or for a year. And let's say that in the intervening days of the week, he demonstrates an authentic appreciation for his spouse, which makes it clear that the flowers are just an extra and not the *only way* he expresses his affection. That's what it takes to convince organizations that are new to this approach. But if you are consistent, and if you are not leaning on the flowers and bagels as the only means of celebrating and showing affection, then it is only a matter of time before employees are won over.

When I would travel in my role as vice president of HR for SAS Institute, two things consistently amazed me. First, if someone were meeting me for the first time, they would often find a way to express to me that they were surprised to find a tough (I'm told!), bottom-line driven fellow in the HR role at a company that famously treated its employees well and regularly ended up on national best-places-to-work lists. They expected a softer personality; maybe even a touchy-feely guy. What these people didn't understand is that for everything we implemented at SAS Institute, we had to have a business rationale to get it approved by the top leadership. We didn't "give away" live music and free M&Ms, nor build café-style eateries, and offer on-site health care *only* to express our affection for our employees. We did it because their care and commitment to the company and its business goals earned that kind of affection. We did it also because it made the workplace a pleasurable and positive environment. As a result we averaged 3 percent voluntary turnover at SAS Institute for years, which was nearly 20 percent better than the industry average. With 7,000 employees worldwide at that time, this *alone* saved SAS Institute tens of millions of dollars each year. And that can pay for a lot of extras. (Keep in mind that it costs 150 percent the salary of a talented person to replace that person and train that replacement.) So, although we were genuinely attuned to our employees, cheered them, and treated them decently, fairly, and like adults, we also undertook activities that were saving the organization vast sums of money with expenditures that may have, at first, looked like country club frills.

The second thing that amazed me when I was traveling during my SAS tenure was this: Many people would come up to me and ask, "What's in those M&Ms at SAS!? How does that type of thing convert into employee loyalty and outstanding business success?" These comments usually spiked in volume when SAS had ended up on one of the best-places-to-work lists. I can't tell you how many times I tried to make the point, without much success, that it wasn't the M&Ms. I tried to disabuse one person after another of the notion that we were buying loyalty with candy. For anyone patient enough to listen I would point out that the M&Ms, the family flex time, indeed *all* the things we did for our employees at SAS were part of a fabric, per se, where each thread was woven into that company fabric that expressed our appreciation for our employees, that cheerlead their accomplishments, that said to them loudly, "You are a valued person. You are important to us, and we want to pay attention to the things that are important to you. We like you and the way you work. We want you to keep doing what you're doing."

Believe me, it wasn't just the M&Ms. Though, to tell you the truth, the peanut M&Ms are slightly addictive.

8

Build a Workplace on a Foundation of Respect

Even the most casual observer can see that people work very well in an atmosphere of high camaraderie, where there is a genuine "niceness" to the work environment. People also seem to thrive and succeed in an atmosphere that fosters respect for *the person*. Moreover, humans need to "belong," and the need to satisfy individual social needs has gravitated to the workplace. Consciously or unconsciously, employees now place a great deal of importance on how the workplace makes them feel about themselves as they go about their daily tasks. Indeed, there is a high expectation of the value of social networking in the workplace. So, it logically follows that the quality of a workplace's social network plays a large role in workplace synergy and therefore, productivity. In fact, when you go to work these days, you are not just going to work. In many ways, you are visiting your "extended family," you are going to your club, and a high-quality social network in the workplace is critical to keep employees engaged. With so much tied to the workplace, a respectful environment where employees honor one another—and are respected in return—is crucial to fostering productive, engaged employees.

Where do you think employees will look for an example of how to treat each other? Well, a respectful tone for employee-to-employee relations is set by leadership and management. That's who employees look to for behavioral role models. By acting respectfully to the people who work for the company, the leadership and management plant the seed of expectation for employees to treat others well. If you don't think that's true, ask yourself if *the opposite* has been true any place you have worked. I'd bet each and every one of us can come up with half a dozen examples. When your leader or manager is disrespectful or abusive, she is sending a loud message that it's okay for you to treat others that way, too. And believe me—for good or ill—that message is picked up in the workplace, just as quickly as it was picked up in your grade school playground, high school gym class, or college dorm.

Another risk of not giving and demanding respect is that an organization can become politicized—that is, split into differing camps. The great danger of a politicized work environment is the same danger any culture faces in a politicized environment, whether that culture is a workplace culture or a national culture. You are destined for decline when ideas and initiatives are not judged on their merits but on the personal allegiances of people within the organization.

Historically, it's obvious how this has damaged nation states, going back to the declining Holy Roman Empire in 500AD. As much as we like to give ourselves credit, human nature hasn't changed all that much since then. In highly politicized environments, if awards, positions, and resources are not awarded on the basis of merit, a number of things will happen, all of them bad. First, you are not likely to achieve success and positive outcomes, because bad ideas are allowed to flourish and drain resources, while sapping morale. Second, when employees see that good ideas and initiatives are left in the dust, while the ideas of the boss's golf buddies are promoted, even though they clearly lack merit, people get demoralized. They not only stop being productive, but they stop putting forth bright ideas, because they know the fate of those ideas won't be decided on merit. Third, those employees—defeated and demoralized—act with resentment to the organization, even to the point of sabotaging its success. Next, they start looking elsewhere for work, leaving the company to wallow in an increasingly toxic, buddy-backslapping system that spirals ever downward. Believe me, I've seen it happen. Employees revert to a survival mentality, where the only way to succeed is to crawl over the back of the person ahead of them. They develop a distrust of the organization ("How could this supposedly great company allow this to happen!?"). They develop a distrust of each other and—worst of all—they become individuals rather than members of a team.

Back in my dot-com days, I saw a prime example of this. The company I was working with had rolled up 12 other software companies, with the intent of digitizing purchase order systems and optimizing the supply chain. By the time anyone looked up long enough to count what was in the till, the amalgamated dot-com company was underwater. One of the companies we had acquired had a supposedly hotshot CEO, and he got up in front of everyone—around 1,200 employees, all told—and said he was a turnaround specialist who was going to save the ship. Problem is, the only people he trusted to save the ship—without exception—were the lieutenants that were already on his team before his company was acquired. Everyone was eager to trust this fellow, and he had the goodwill of everyone in that meeting. But he couldn't have handled it more poorly. He took away most of the power from an able middle management team, treated everyone who wasn't from his tribe as though they were stupid children, and stopped returning phone calls. It wasn't long before he'd lost the faith of the other employees, and *everything* he or his team did was suspect. *Everything.* Good or bad. People grew so full of contempt for his disregard and lack of communication, they ended up in some cases actively working against the actions that would ensure the company's survival and their very jobs!

Why?

Well, let me break this argument down a bit more, so I can define the causes of the problem more specifically and show the various ways to give and demand respect, because that is the key to understanding the dot-com story I just related.

I am from Pittsburgh, Pennsylvania, and I spent my childhood there. When I was growing up as part of a large Italian family, I could walk to the homes of closest relatives, including my aunts and uncles, cousins, and grandparents. This experience wasn't necessary unique to our community with Italian heritage (though I take great pride in knowing without a doubt that we of all cultures ate the best food!). Seriously, this was a common cultural phenomenon when I was growing up as a child in the 1940s and 50s. All the immigrant families created tight social networks. It was a family tradition that relatives dropped by each other's homes during the week. We gathered for church on Sundays, and after church we would have a family meal that turned into a weekly family social. We teased each other, we gave each other advice, we argued, we commiserated. We had a close and robust family network.

The family next to us was German, and they engaged in the same behavior with their extended family. The family on the other side of us was Irish, and they too engaged each other this way. But today, I'm somewhat sad to admit, these classic nuclear families just don't exist. I have heard it said that in the United States the closest relative, not living under the same roof, lives, on average, 120 miles away.

The breakdown of the family social fabric and nuclear family structure that I experienced as a child did not somehow vacate the emotional need that the family structure provided. In fact, in Maslow's hierarchy of human needs, the third most-demanding need is the social need to belong to something, to be able to act not just as an individual, but as part of a group.

What social institution do you think has replaced the family social fabric and nuclear family structure? It's the workplace. The workplace has re-created and replaced the social networks many baby boomers experienced as children. Instead of going to a family gathering or a club, we go to work. That's where our *club* meets everyday. Workmates are our extended family, and—in addition to the family activities that we still engage in with our blood relatives, often over the phone or the Internet—we engage with our extended "family" at work in much the same way we used to engage with our extended family 40 or 50 years ago. We seek advice, we commiserate, we support each other, we play, we argue—and we trust each other.

With that in mind, leaders and managers of today's organizations need to recognize this dynamic. Even more than that, they have to demonstrate a keen understanding of the role the workplace plays in the social fabric of their employees and their families. Leaders and managers need to show respect *for* that reality, and show respect for individuals in the workplace *because of* that reality.

I am not saying that the workplace has to be like a social club. After all, work has to be done; tasks must be accomplished without too many social distractions. But leaders and managers have to acknowledge that the workplace is not just a place where work gets done, and their policies must reflect that acknowledgement. Properly implemented, policies of a mindful leader or manager can take advantage of this reality and improve productivity as a result. How? By building a human and physical infrastructure that has high social value. By building an infrastructure for work *as a social activity*.

Indeed, the workplace must be seen as a crucible for social networking.

If you are not following me to this point, let me say that building an infrastructure for work *as a social activity* isn't a matter of arranging the work cubicles in an open interlocking pattern or having beanbag chairs around the coffee area. Though your approach may end up including open cubicles and beanbag chairs, creating a human infrastructure for work *as a social activity* requires far more than those steps. It's a matter of fostering an emotional environment where leaders and managers contribute to a high-quality social network. To do that, leaders and managers need to demand of themselves and of their employees the creation of a social atmosphere where people lift each other up. (Do you think the CEO rescue hotshot was prepared to act this way in saving the dot-com? Nope. Never crossed his mind.)

Moreover, leaders and managers need to oversee these efforts protectively, just as a strong paternal figure oversees a large family. That can be as simple as putting basic rules of interaction in place: Be respectful of people you disagree with. Be caring. Find paths to turn disagreements and arguments into positive outcomes by working toward clearly communicated common goals. Ask employees to discover the purity and genuineness of each other's intentions, even in conflicting situations. Indeed, the leader or manager should try to create synergies that *wouldn't otherwise exist* to propel the company forward, and finally to create and equitably distribute tangible and intangible awards to recognize high performance.

A question that may naturally occur at this point is: How does leadership act to give permission to their employees to act civilly and positively toward each other? Well, one thing I know for sure is that you don't stop answering your phone. Or freezing people out. In his book *In Search of Excellence*, Tom Peters states that this kind of work environment can be achieved through "management by walking around." This means that the manager must create a personal relationship with the employees. He's got to come out of his ivory tower on a regular basis, to meet and talk with the people who work there.

This isn't accomplished through cold and dictatorial memos or broadcasts, but through the creation and strengthening of social networks. It's often just a matter of listening. Or asking, "What are you doing, and how is it going?" Or of the leader or manager asking, "What can I do to make this place a better place to work? What can I do to foster your productivity?"

A few years ago, I was brought in by a division head at American Express who was aware of my work at SAS Institute. He asked me what American Express could do to foster better communication and a feeling of teamwork among the employees. They were also interested in making the employees feel as though they were part of a family, under the correct assumption that this would drive up productivity. In my engagement, the first thing I addressed was American Express's desire to move a particular metric about employee's negative impression of management from 15 percent to 0 percent in one year. I told them that they might be able to do that, but it would likely spring back, as dramatic "movements of the needle" in one year usually aren't sustainable. I suggested trying to move it 5 percent the first year, and another 5 percent the second year, and so on. And what policies did I recommend that they use?

Doughnuts. That's right, I suggested that they use doughnuts in a regularly scheduled employee-management meeting.

The doughnuts weren't a reward *per se*, or an incentive. But they would provide an opportunity for the management to listen to their employees. The management might not take all (or any) of the employees' suggestions to heart. Some might work; some might not. Some employees may not be aware of the long-term strategic implications of some of their suggestions in the overarching scheme of American Express's future plans. But it's the *act of listening* that engenders a positive link from the employees to the management. The *act of listening* is a way of showing respect, or openly and publicly stating: Hey, we care about you, and we give permission for you to care about and listen to each other, just as we are caring about and listening to you. (I refer to this as the $15,000 doughnut dozen, because that's how much American Express could have saved if they'd just bought the doughnuts from around the corner, opened their ears to their employees, and skipped hiring me!)

Even with the doughnuts, and the management by walking around, other things must be consistent through these activities and methods of outreach: An authentic and sincere vibe from leaders and managers that the employees' opinions and workplace environment matters to them and to the company; that the leaders and managers treat employees decently, as adults, and expect the same in return; that leaders and management respect the contribution of team players; and that leaders freely distribute *atta boys* and *atta girls* where they are earned and deserved are all important contributors. Sometimes this means listening. Sometimes this means speaking loudly. But it *always* means being human, honest, sincere, and available.

The next crucial activity of a leader or manager is to ensure that every person who *comes into* the team is critical to camaraderie, and that the removal of every team member who is *moved out* of the team results in the potential for increased camaraderie, as well. In that sense, the leader or manager has to be sensitive to what would disrupt the social dynamic of the team, and balance the team members accordingly. This certainly means that leaders and managers must be quick to act when recognizing and removing people who are toxic. The toxic effect of bad employees obviously has a negative effect on social networks and team dynamics. But when a leader or manager knowingly leaves a toxic person on a team, he is also signaling that he doesn't care about the team, that the team can tough it out; like it or lump it. Ignoring that sort of problem is nothing short of a measure of disrespect.

To finish out this chapter, I have to preface this chapter's last anecdote by saying how blessed I was to work for a flame-out dot-com. In my short time there, I picked up so much material for this book, *far disproportionate* to the material I picked up at SAS Institute in my 19 years there. That said, there was this fellow who joined us at the dot-com, and he was brought in to unify the sales effort across 12 acquired companies. He was immediately suspect, in my opinion, because he was good friends with a powerful member of our board. So, right away, I recognized that this was possibly a political appointment and perhaps, just perhaps, not based on the merit of the man. But he had a killer resume, with an international banking and data background, and I initially gave him the benefit of the doubt, as I do for most people.

But signs of his toxicity popped up immediately. He made it clear that he thought he was smarter than everyone else there. Now, I recognize that some people are smarter than others, but the smartest people I know are the least likely to assert themselves in this way; they just let the brilliance shine through on an event-by-event basis, until everyone sooner or later recognizes that they are dealing with someone special. This fellow's braggart behavior was Strike Two in my book.

This fellow also made no bones about telling people he was in it for the money and that he didn't really care whether the company did well or not. He was just going to hang on until the IPO and scram. Strike Three.

But it only got worse. And he had no strikes left!

This fellow was a polarizer who thought that progress was made by pitting people against one another, in some brutal form of a Darwinism of ideas. People who were "with him" (recognized his brilliance) were celebrated; they could do no wrong, and they were given vast latitude to stretch and break rules. People who were against him (people who questioned his decisions) were dismissed and ignored, if not actively and publicly talked down. This guy was the classic toxic boss. People widely developed a dislike for him, as it became increasingly clear he wasn't going to decide anything on the merits of an idea, but on the personal relationship he had with his chosen team of favorites and sycophants. Many veteran employees—seasoned corporate players and responsible adults—told me that they'd never seen a more toxic and politicized work environment. And still this toxic fellow plugged on.

The problem didn't stop with this fellow's management style and its ensuing ineffectiveness. He contaminated the workplace with disrespect. But *the inaction of leadership* to manage this guy was just as much an act of disrespect for the employees as the toxic man himself. The leadership, whose jobs and initiatives were funded or defunded at the ultimate discretion of the board, was fearful of going against a board member's favored choice for VP of sales.

Well, that lasted until management couldn't deny that this man was *so* toxic, coupled with a mass movement (the wisdom of the crowds of people who really were getting something done) to get rid of this guy, and he was finally fired. So vainglorious was this man that as part of his departure he insisted on writing a farewell e-mail to all 1,200 employees of the company to say that his "decision to depart was not taken lightly." But everyone knew he was fired, and they snickered when reading the e-mail. That feeling of triumph and relief *alone* among the employees probably got the dot-com to last another six months beyond its natural lifetime. It generated a feeling of mutual respect, it showed that the employees' opinions were valued and acted on, even to the point of firing a so-called hotshot senior executive who the "wise crowds" saw early on as nothing more than a windbag.

9

Cultivate the Risk-Trust Dynamic

Employees must trust management and, reciprocally, management must trust employees. Case study after case study shows that where there is trust, "great places to work" can flourish. As I talked about in earlier chapters, great places to work are *not* the organizations that become famous for putting out bowls of free M&Ms or letting employees take extra personal days. Historically, great places to work are organizations where the culture of engaged employees—and the policies that sustain and engage them—creates a competitive advantage, lower turnover, consistent stock growth, and market share growth. And a key workplace component that underpins all of these is trust.

Trust is nothing more than the willingness of a person to be vulnerable, the willingness to give of herself. The more an employee trusts someone—a coworker, a boss—the more she allows her preferred self to emerge. (The *preferred self* is that person who emerges when there is alignment between the person's personal attributes and the organization's goals.) And as Martha Stewart might say, "And that's a good thing." The emergence of a preferred self is an essential quality—if not *the* essential quality—of an engaged and highly productive employee. Let's look a little deeper at trust, what it means specifically, and how to foster it in the workplace.

Given how trust is key to a successful business, it may seem to be an ephemeral topic, something hard to define and even harder to create. But you may be surprised to learn that quite a bit of research has been done on how to foster trust, and on the detriments and draw-backs of a workplace that lacks trust.

The Great Place to Work Institute was founded in San Francisco in 1991 by Robert Levering and Amy Lyman. The work of the institute springs from decades of research that Robert Levering and Milton Moskowitz first published in their 1984 book *The 100 Best Companies to Work for in America*. Not long ago, the Great Place to Work Institute put forth consensus attributes of great places to work. The institute says that the first element that makes a great place to work is that the work itself is interesting and challenging. Second, there is a high level of camaraderie in the workplace. And third, an overarching, high level of trust operates in the workplace at all times.

The Great Place to Work Institute defines trust in two ways. First, there is the trust that management displays. This is the trust that management has in its people. This trust is expressed through the day-to-day behavior of management, and that behavior must be a model for what management expects of its employees to 1) behave in high quality ways, 2) work hard on behalf of the company, 3) produce goods and services at highest quality, 4) maintain honest relations with clients and customers *and each other*, and 5) provide input and ideas that propel the company forward to achieve competitive advantage. That my sound a little dry and academic, so let me put it to you plainly: A "great-place environment" is dependent on the entirely novel idea that leaders and managers should treat their employees as if they are all big boys and big girls who have brains. They should treat their employees as capable and worthy. They should treat them as though they are members of a team, rather than hired hands. Too simple a concept to be effective? Read on.

It's not that hard to foster this kind of workplace culture, because it is not about policies and protocols, but human behavior. Let me give you an example. When workers are trained at the Four Seasons Hotels, one central tenet of that training—one of the foundations by which all their on-the-job behavior should be judged—is this motto or slogan: *We are ladies and gentlemen serving ladies and gentleman.*

Any action that an employee takes should be seen in light of that motto. When a hotel guest asks for extra help, the employee's response should be what a lady or gentleman would do for another lady or gentlemen. It's not about policies or protocols; it's about behavior.

Now, when a company is trying to be a great place to work, that atmosphere can be fostered when people ask themselves—before each and every action, until it becomes a habit—is this how I should behave to a member of my team? Is this how I should behave to a thinking and considerate adult? Is this how I should act toward someone capable and worthy of trust? If the answer is yes, then the behavior is proper, and it's *not* something that you have to check in a reference manual.

Next, this trust needs to flow from leaders and managers to employees, but it also must flow back from employees. The employees must trust that the leadership is acting with the company's and the employee's best interests in mind, even if it may not seem so with some decisions, at first blush. That trust isn't always easy to earn (or maintain), but the employees have to trust that the leadership cares about them, not only as a means to an end (for example, profit and enduring competitive advantage), but as *people*. And leadership must demonstrate that it cares about what its people care about, too.

When you have this dynamic, where trust is shared on a two-way street (employee-to-employer and employer-to-employee), the workplace welcomes an atmosphere of accountability and ownership. On the one hand, employees have a reason to feel responsible for outcomes *and* for sustaining this sense of trust by taking actions that are worthy of trust. On the other hand, the more the leader or manager is able to trust, the less inclined he is to micromanage the employee. When the trust dynamic is working particularly well, it only accelerates. As employees demonstrate more and more reason to be trusted, more and more trust is granted. As leaders grant more and more trust, employees take more and more ownership of their roles and outcomes, because they know that there is not a backstop; there is no one playing behind them, no one there to correct their errors. This is the workplace dynamic that breeds leaders—leaders who are brought up from within, *not* leaders who are brought in from outside just for their skills. (Those kinds of leaders must be acculturated to the new workplace environment, at great cost of time and money and at *gross* costs of time and money if the acculturation proves impossible.)

For leaders who are freed of the onus of micromanagement, and who know that they can look the other way and not be taken advantage of, they too are freed to engage in activities that leaders are supposed to do, activities that can truly give a company competitive advantage. Not babysitting. Not dreaming up punishments. Not patrolling the hallways looking for people who are coming back late from lunch. But being creative and imaginative in future planning and process optimization. Cheerleading. Managing by walking around.

In workplace environments like that, where the trust factor is very high, when "the nickel stands on its edge" the management and leadership will push it over to the side that favors the employees, and conversely, when that nickel stands on its edge, the employees will push it over to the side that favors the company.

The next natural question is this: How do you create an atmosphere where trust emerges? First, you have to establish a workplace philosophy that assumes the following: Employees are not there to cheat or to be on the dole. In fact, leaders and managers have to trust that employees are there to make a contribution. Think back to Theory X and Theory Y Management, which I wrote about earlier in this book. Take to heart the fact that many people want to be led, yet they don't want to be overly supervised. Accordingly, leaders and managers must look at their people not as assets to be policed and lorded over, but as resources capable of helping the organization achieve great competitive advantage, which also works to everyone's personal advantage as well.

To achieve this, leaders and managers have to be trustworthy. They have to establish patterns of doing the things that they say they are going to do; they have to follow through. It's no different from the way you react to people in your personal life, is it? If someone repeatedly lets you down on promises, you develop doubt and mistrust. If you are in a bind and their promises really must be carried through on, your natural inclination is to reach in, call, prod, and micromanage, because you distrust their ability to follow through. The same is true in the workplace. When leaders or managers say they are going to get something done, they'd better follow through. Otherwise the employees quickly develop cynicism and distrust for "just another empty promise from management." This means leaders and managers must be consistent and transparent.

Second in building trust, leaders have to communicate the truth of the business situation, and, accordingly, they have to be clear when communicating what they expect from the people. You might notice that many of the best places to work in America are often organizations that have transparent processes, decision making, and even financials. The leadership lays it all out there: where the organization is against goal, how well it did last month, what must be achieved by each department to achieve the next goal. That's a key element for fostering teamwork, trust, and camaraderie.

Does this mean that leaders and managers have to be Pollyannas? Or Little Miss Sunshines? No. But they have to cheerlead, be consistent, be highly communicative, and request the behaviors that will achieve outcomes valuable to the organization.

Contrary to what some of you might think, creating trust has little to do with money. Money has value, but it doesn't have core value, and it doesn't ensure cultural value. After all, who would turn down money? You give it away; people are going to take it. You give them bonus checks; they are going to cash them. However, with or without the bonus checks, employees sense whether leadership cares about them, based on how much trust has been engendered in the workplace environment. In an environment where there is mistrust, the bonus checks are just like that one-time bouquet of flowers, the dozen bagels that turn out to be a fluke. They are just empty symbols.

Let's drill down a little more and take a closer look at the nature of trust.

As valuable as trust is, it is nothing more than the ability for someone to be vulnerable. When I say vulnerable, I don't mean in a manner of psychological immaturity. Instead, I mean that you are open. That you accept suggestions and don't mind when people expect things of you. It means not getting defensive when criticized, because you don't feel threatened at your core in any real way. You feel secure, even when your work is questioned, because the questioning is done with the goal to improve the competitive position and productivity of the company through your work, not to call into doubt your motives or intentions. In these settings, your preferred self can emerge, because you know that your open trusting self isn't going to be attacked or stabbed in the back. And when you are this open, it frees you up to do the work without distraction. All of your capabilities can be applied, and you can become absorbed in your work. That's when people produce their best, because their own sense of pride in their work is being exercised and exerted for themselves, for their teams, and for the advancement of the business goals of the organization. Every tier, every layer of the workplace environment is in sync, including the emotional and physical intelligence of the employee.

Not to get too idealistic about this or to imply that this trusting disposition is heaven on earth and easy to sustain, but maybe you have been blessed to feel this way at one time or another in your life. You hear from professional athletes that they were "in the zone," or that "the ball seemed larger than usual." "The hoop seemed bigger." "I couldn't miss." "All the noise fell away."

In the workplace all the "noise" that falls away in an atmosphere of trust is the office politics, the micromanagement, the suspicion. And it can produce spectacular results. Try it, and see.

Let me ask you something: Would the activities, actions, and behaviors I am suggesting in this chapter cause a wave of disbelief in your workplace? If your workplace has an element of mistrust, then these actions by leadership and management—if implemented suddenly and with no follow-through—would indeed cause disbelief.

Remember the story I told in an earlier chapter about the fellow in a ho-hum relationship who unexpectedly brings home flowers? Or the company leader who suddenly brings in bagels? The first time you do this, everyone will be waiting for the bad news, the layoffs, the budget cuts. But if leaders and managers are consistent, and the actions they take to foster trust are not done just once and never revisited, but consistently publicly stated and backed up with action, *then* you will start to win over your employees. Moreover, by announcing your intention to foster trust, it's like writing a promise to your spouse or business partner and taping it in a prominent place. It's a public statement. It can be referred to as a reminder. It increases the pressure for leaders and managers to live up to what you have promised, or risk wide condemnation. If leaders and managers announce, "We're going to do this! Please watch us. Guide us. Challenge us. This is our stake in the ground." That's when you begin to gain credence among your workforce, a credence that is affirmed and built on by consistent action and consistently clear communication.

Companies that do this badly are the ones that try the flavor of the month and are not consistent and disciplined. Metaphorically, these are like people who jump from fad diet to fad diet, never sticking to one consistent approach that would achieve the desired outcome: losing weight. And what's the result of that? Discouragement, defeatism, and the abandonment of the cause. These types of companies are unwilling, unaware, or just plain incapable of revising their philosophy about people in the workplace.

One more SAS story to wrap up this chapter. Years ago, when we were putting together our corporate policies at SAS, we decided that we would not have a time clock (for punching in and out) and we would not have a sick leave policy, with a set number of sick days allotted to each employee. Sounds crazy, right? It may have seemed to others that we were reckless with our trust and setting ourselves up for abuse, especially with the sick leave policy. But our feeling was this: If you're sick, you're sick, and you should stay home. We announced the "no-policy policy" and let it be known that we "trusted" our people to behave responsibly and as adults, with the expectation that it would not be abused. We provided lots of freedom with equal responsibility—with a reminder of the reality of less-than-adult behavior—"be absent for five or six consecutive Mondays or Fridays, and expect to be dismissed."

The principle behind this policy was that we trusted our employees to behave and act as adults. However, we also recognized that employees who call in sick when they are not sick obviously want to be somewhere else. And believe me, we gave a couple of people the *permanent* chance to be or work somewhere else. We found that the vast majority of people responded very well to this approach. The more we treated them as adults, the more they acted like adults. SAS experienced consistently low absenteeism. Beyond how the policy was received (and it is still in place and working today), this approach goes back to the Montessori approach, which we put in place at SAS's day-care and child-care facilities. We gave SAS employees a great deal of freedom, but we made it clear that freedom came with responsibility—the responsibility to themselves, to their coworkers, and to the company. We expressed our trust, and we were repaid with trust, enduring loyalty, and much more.

A final word on trust and lack of trust in the workplace as seen through a major federal government intrusion into the prerogatives that companies have to deal with the people they employ. Prior to the passage of the Family Medical Leave Act in 1993, many companies had sick leave policies that provided for paid or unpaid time off for employees who were too ill to come to work. However, few companies had provisions in these policies to allow employees to stay at home to care for a sick child or other close relative. To stay at home for other than personal illness was a clear violation of policy and subject to disciplinary action. Nonetheless, many employees, with few alternatives available to them, called in sick to care for a sick child or relative, knowingly violating policy. Many were caught; some were terminated.

Some of these employees saw this as wrongful discharge, found lawyers, moved the complaint up the food chain to Congress, and Voila!, the Family Medical Leave Act. And, for me, the root of all this is a pattern of distrust that began when companies treated employees as though they would abuse any privilege.

10

Make Room for Fun in the Workplace (Nurture Lightheartedness/Levity)

A few months ago I was traveling on an American Airlines flight between Chicago and home. As luck would have it, I was served a cup of sparkling water by a very pleasant, smiling, and chatty cabin attendant. Looking for something to read, I pulled the house magazine, *American Way*, from the seat-back pocket. As I scanned the contents of the periodical, my attention was drawn to a one-page review of a business book written to promote levity in the workplace. The book was described as a call to companies and their leaders to "lighten up."

The review was appealing, and it brought back a memory of my earliest days in corporate America. I was 25 years old and working for Westinghouse Electric Company within the commercial Nuclear Energy Division as an HR newbie. I must have been full of the joy of landing a real job, with real pay, at a place where many other young folks worked. We had a brand-new building, with walls painted bright primary colors and a glass and steel façade. I was loving it, and it showed. A group of us would meet regularly for pre-workday coffee (I took my caffeine in the form of Diet Pepsi), had lunch together, and occasionally stopped into a local pub for a beer or cocktail after work to wait out the commuter traffic.

As far as I can remember most of us in the group were committed to doing good work, and most of us were satisfactory-or-better contributors, and at some level we all showed potential for advancement. But, we had a good time at work, too. There was a lot smiling, chatting in the halls, playful teasing, sports and fashion talk, and general spreading of goodwill, all laced in between accomplishing tasks and delivering on objectives.

For some reason, my manager's manager, a division director, saw me as both a "high potential" employee and the Pied Piper of this happy group. So, late one afternoon, he summoned me to his corner office (with windows that overlooked the Pennsylvania Turnpike—nature at its best) for a "chat." His word, not mine. He sat behind his desk with his pipe *(A word about pipes a little later)*, which alternated between his teeth and his hands for packing and repacking. He told me that I had a great future ahead of me. But, he said, I was at risk of throwing it all away because of my behavior at work.

I was riveted to my seat, as I asked the nature of my transgressions.

He leaned toward me and offered that the managers were beginning to think that I was not serious about my job and not behaving professionally. So, being the person my father and mother had raised, I asked to hear the evidence against me. He told me that I smiled all the time, and I was seen to be far too "loose and casual" to be serious about my job and my work.

Anyway, I really thought he was kidding. But he wasn't! You see, I was among others behaving counterintuitively to the management. They believed deeply that work was serious stuff, not to be "played with." Any regular show of joy or levity that was outside organized social events indicated a lack of seriousness and care, and it was considered nonprofessional. *Basically, if you are having a good time at work, you can't be getting anything done.*

It took me one week to decide to look elsewhere for work, but I checked out long before I physically moved on 15 months later.

Thank God, the days of smoking in the workplace were numbered. But I sometimes wonder if the old guy had a legitimate point. Because as I recall my days at Westinghouse, the guy who read me the riot act certainly never plowed up new ground when it came to accomplishments and contribution.

Now, a word about pipes, if you will excuse the intrusion into this space. About 35 years ago, I was promoted into my first real management role, where I could actually hire and fire people. Well, my division director took me out for a welcoming lunch, and over coffee (Diet Pepsi still for me), he offered this sage advice, "Never hire a pipe smoker! They spend all their time loading, packing, lighting, relighting, emptying, cleaning, and repeating the sequence. They may look smart and serious, but they never get anything done!

What I Learned from Marie Montessori

Twelve years later, I had the best kind of learning experience, dealing with this same subject. It was "discovery learning"; you know, one of those times when you learn something that is so cool and eye-opening that it stays with you forever, where the news is not brought to you, but rather you find it yourself, much like a paleontologist turns over a rock and discovers a rare fossil.

When I was head of HR at SAS Institute (now called SAS), and we were expanding our benefits options, one of the possibilities we considered was adding on-site day care for infants, toddlers, and preschoolers to support our growing complement of working mothers and young two-career families.

As we interviewed companies and independent day-care providers in our search for a day-care solution that would fit our need, values, and culture, we asked our employees, who would be the beneficiaries of our choice, for any information they may have had access to that could help us. One of our young mothers suggested that we consider establishing a Montessori Day Care and Preschool, and she even suggested a person who could serve as director of the center and lead teacher.

We obliged and brought the outside specialist in for an interview to discuss what Montessori had to offer SAS and its families. It turns out that the Montessori method of child development offered much to SAS, and I was totally enlightened by what I learned that day, and by what I have learned and retained as a "values touchstone" for more than 25 years since.

At SAS we prided ourselves on building and nurturing a healthy and creative work environment. We believed and behaved as though people—given the right resources, guidance, and infrastructure, *and* the appropriate amounts of encouragement and recognition—would amaze us with the things they could and would do on behalf of the company. Well, to my surprise and joy, an Italian physician, Maria Montessori, was way ahead of us. Back before the turn of the twentieth century, Montessori, who died in 1952, was showing the world, or at least Europe, that creativity is fostered in children (and that learning and achievement are enhanced) in environments where high expectations are set and where there is a rigid infrastructure. But the approach is a balancing act, because the infrastructure cannot be too burdensome. People must be encouraged to take their own leads to achievement *and be cheered for it.* This is all done with the assumption that the outcomes are aligned and do not violate the established infrastructure.

So what does this and Maria Montessori have to do with levity (fun!) in the workplace. Well, it happens that one of Maria's principles (I view her as an old friend now...I wonder if she prepared gnocchi from scratch?) is that work is fun and should be fun; play is fun and should be fun. They are just different kinds of fun. She believed and showed that when work is done without joy there is less creativity, less engagement, and far less productivity. So, your goal as a manager is to lead people to a place where learning and work are joyful experiences. The result is that satisfaction comes from achievement, and the quality and volume of the outcome is enhanced. Moreover, the creativity applied to the tasks builds learning, which, in turn, virtually guarantees better results—and more "fun"—in the future.

In Rule 1, "Understand Why Employees Come and Why They Stay," I referred to Douglas McGregor's Theory X and Theory Y Management. McGregor was a professor at the MIT Sloan School of Management, and in his book *The Human Side of the Enterprise*, he indentified these two approaches to management. With Theory X Management it was assumed that people needed to be managed, pushed, and supervised. It assumed that without management, people wouldn't produce *at all* unless there was a risk that something would be taken away from them.

With Theory Y management, the management orientation was focused on the practical application of Maslow's hierarchy of human needs. Theory Y assumed that work comes as naturally to people as play, and moreover, if people are given the right guidance, resources, and encouragement, they will *naturally* produce, and do so very well, with positive outcomes.

To put this in a more common vernacular, Theory X management believes that people, at their core, are lazy and need to be pushed, whereas Theory Y management assumes the opposite, that people are naturally curious and productive, and when they are put in the right place, with the right resources, they will be successful.

Okay, at the risk of causing an explosion, let's combine McGregor and Montessori. All kidding aside, they are remarkably similar: Montessori and McGregor assume that there can be levity in the workplace and in learning environments, and that levity is the *natural disposition* of ideal work and educational settings!

So, how valuable can having fun be? Herb Kelleher, cofounder and two-time CEO of Southwest Airlines, was intent on making his company a fun place to be. He believed that customer service was at the core of any successful business. And he also believed that employees provide the best customer service when they are having fun doing their work. So he and Colleen Barrett, his longtime number-one assistant (who eventually took a turn as Southwest's president herself), insisted that the Southwest hiring process include a test of an applicant's sense of humor. Each applicant was asked to stand up and tell a joke before the panel of interviewers. Now, was this a test to see who was funny or could deliver a punch line? Nope! Southwest was looking for people who would be able to take the job seriously, but not themselves; people who would be comfortable and thrive in an atmosphere that required a lot of teamwork and camaraderie; and who would embrace being externally focused toward the customers and other employees. They were also looking for candidates who found joy in life and saw the glass perpetually half full. Think it has worked in Southwest's favor? You bet.

So leaders are wise to introduce fun into the workplace and to foster lightheartedness. Executives certainly don't have to be funny or lead the joke telling. It is far more important that executives and managers are pleasant to be around. And one can be a hard-working, driven, and demanding taskmaster, and still be a person with a pleasant demeanor.

In fact, as we found at SAS, and as you will find by implementing the principles in this book, fun in the workplace is not mutually exclusive to productivity. Indeed, one actually *enhances* the other, and having fun in the workplace isn't necessarily an indication that little work is getting done—as long as the fun isn't reckless and doesn't violate the values, mission, or established company infrastructure.

What's more, when that sense of fun is in the workplace, the extraordinary becomes common. Why? Because everyone can be so *in the zone* that extraordinary acts come naturally to them. By analogy, think of what people say after they have performed a rescue of some kind. It seems as tough they invariably say "it wasn't anything heroic, just something anyone would do."

They are in the zone, and the extraordinary seems common.

Think of sports figures who put in amazing performances—like Magic Johnson. Remember his *rookie year*? Game 7 of the playoffs, and Kareem has a migraine. Magic plays center—not his natural position—and effortlessly pours in 40 points to lead the Los Angeles Lakers to the championship. That night, he looked as though he was having a blast, and I am sure he was. He was immersed. In the zone. The extraordinary came naturally.

You hear the same thing about artists. They get so immersed in their work that they go without sleeping or eating. This can go on for days at a time, and yet when they are asked if the work was hard, they look up baffled, as if to say, "I didn't think it was work at all. I was having fun."

I know it seems idealistic to assume you can expect constant peak performance, heroic acts, and spectacular individual contribution on a daily basis, but you can build and sustain a workplace environment where these feats are possible. And that's half the battle.

11

Create Opportunities for Employee "Alignment" with Vision, Values, and Mission

To cultivate truly engaged employees, organizations need to build "linking opportunities" between an organization's wants, needs, and culture and the issues that drive employees and garner their attention, passion, and care. Think *visceral*! Obviously, one of the first steps for creating alignment is for leaders to get to know their employees at a deep level. I know that sounds intrusive and presumptive, but it should be simple and obvious. It's almost patronizing to state that again here, but you'd be surprised how really uncommon it is for leadership to be "in the know" about what makes the workforce tick.

Try it yourself. Right now. Can you name two or three issues that are consistently and specifically important to your employees in general? Those things that generate water cooler talk, raised voices, joy and concern, bonding and sharing? When I say "important," I am talking about the issues that are part of the daily pulse of life—like commuting woes and school board decisions. And I am also talking about larger issues of interest and concern; things like the employees' aspirations for their children, their desires and hopes for themselves, their communities, and their country are central to this theme. Whether it's "going green," or ethics, or the Consumer Price Index, or the state of health care, these are the personal and global concerns that your employees bring to work with them every day.

And, believe it or not, they are watching and listening for action and behavior that indicate where an organization stands, or falls, with regard to these things. In short, they tie their dreams and fears to the way the company perceives and reacts to the worlds around them. This includes both the intimate personal world of family, friends, and future, and the more distant but critically important world of economics and geopolitical events. Now, don't expect any of them to prepare a treatise on these subjects, but understand that your employees are no less the "victims" of the six o'clock news and the dinner table news than you are; and they look to you for pathways to solutions, because you are in the better position to be the champion—you are relatively bigger, richer, smarter, more influential, and more powerful.

It's imperative that members of the C suite know their employees in this way because knowing employees' work-life issues, and their aspirations for personal growth and career development, is the first step toward linking employee aspirations with company goals, finding common causes with your employees. It is the first step toward achieving alignment, with all the distinctive competitive advantages—loyalty, teamwork, productivity—that alignment can bring. When you find that alignment, you arrive and dwell at a place where the organization's goals and values foster ever-deepening links to the employees' personal values, their dreams, objectives, and missions.

One clear path to building linking opportunities is to have an open culture where employees feel they are an integral, essential part of the organization and that they are directly contributing to the organization's goals. When employees are aligned with the organization's values and mission, and the organization displays its respect for individuals, employees engage more actively because they believe that their employer feels and thinks as they do. It's only human nature, isn't it?

Let's look at this on the macro scale with some examples. Take the global pharmaceutical company Merck. It says "The mission of Merck is to provide society with superior products and services by developing innovations and solutions that improve the quality of life and satisfy customer needs, and to provide employees with meaning-ful work and advancement opportunities, and investors with a supe-rior rate of return."

Sounds audacious, doesn't it? Well, it is. But notice that it is not product-focused, like the mission statement from, say, a driven, tech-nology company like Oracle. (You can find Oracle's mission statement on the Web, and it's markedly different in tone and feel from Merck's.)

Dare I say that the Merck mission statement is "aspirational" (that is, it declares what kind of business Merck wants to be); it's even inspirational. Indeed, it's almost touching to see that a large company could express such compassion by stating they want to develop "inno-vations and solutions that improve the quality of life."

Let me ask you another question: Do you think that certain types of people would read this mission statement and say, "Wow, I know I would fit in there!" Certainly. Can you also imagine that certain other types of people would read the mission statement and say, "That place doesn't sound right for me. It's too...*too*. I just want to make money; I don't want to save the world." So the Merck mission state-ment acts simultaneously as a beacon and a lighthouse: One calls cer-tain people, and the other warns people off. And believe me it's just as important to turn an employee *away* with your mission statement as it is to draw the right people. It's far more expensive and time-consuming to hire and fire the wrong person than to wait and hire the right person the first time.

You see, the mission statement is the first step toward defining the terms of an alignment between the organization and the employee. It's the first step toward finding people who are in sync with the company's goals and values, people who feel that the organi-zation's mission is aligned with the kind of company they want to be associated with—the kind of company they want to have their profes-sional legacies linked to.

Here's another example. Johnson & Johnson does not have a mission statement per se, but for more than 60 years it has had a 1,600-word "credo." It is fairly wide-ranging, but you can guess its contents from the tone of the opening sentence, which states, "We believe our first responsibility is to the doctors, nurses and patients, to mothers and fathers and all others who use our products and services."

Here, too, prospective employees can read that and broadly agree or disagree that this is a workplace where their personal goals and the organization's goals can find common cause, to align, and subsequently engage. If you don't believe that your first responsibility at work is to "doctors, nurses and patients, to mothers and fathers," then you won't fit in at J&J, and you should look elsewhere for meaningful work.

Notice that the missions of both of these organizations are externally focused.

That said, the mission statement doesn't have to be altruistic. If asked to articulate a mission statement, some organizations may say that they are "in business to make money." Full stop. They will draw prospective employees who share that value, whatever the consequences to the company years hence.

As with the other aspects of managing companies that I have addressed in this book, the mission statement or credo does not *create* the organization's values. It should describe a culture that *already exists* at the company. Without a doubt, the mission statement or credo can help sustain that culture, but it can't create it. The leadership does that.

You can easily imagine an extreme example, I am sure. You can't be an importing business that buys expired third-world pharmaceuticals for resale to U.S. children, while you issue a credo that says you are "concerned about people's health worldwide." It's empty sloganeering, and employees will be the first to detect that the leadership doesn't stand behind the company's stated principles, which inevitably creates a festering sore that breeds toxic workplaces and contempt. So, your mission statement has to be sincere. It has to articulate a set of values that exist (or that you aspire to diligently subscribe to) at your organization. It can express aspirations; indeed, it *should* declare aspirations, but they must be achievable by the estimation of reasonable people. You can't have a 50-person company that makes specialty tools in Vermont and claim in your mission statement that you are "a global purveyor of a full range of the world's finest tools to leading corporations." No one would believe you, because it's not true, and the employees would be the first to grow cynical about the claim. You can, however, say, "Our team of New England craftsmen aims to delight customers anywhere in the world with a line of fascinating, hand-crafted specialty tools."

Now, here's a to-do—and you have not had much homework in this book *so far*, so stop the bellyaching. Go ahead and write an accurate mission statement or credo for your company as it is today. Be entirely honest, even if your mission statement declares that you are not (yet!) the best in your field. Then, more importantly, write a mission statement or credo for the company you want to be. That second document shows you how far you are in policies and alignment from where you need to be, and it is instructive, in any event.

Elsewhere in this book, I have discussed that one of the reasons people go to work is to learn and grow. So, if you have a company that says that developing your people through learning and growth is a core, defining feature, then declare it to be so in your mission statement. If your company's core value is to be "family friendly," say so. That's something that people can get behind. (Frankly, it would be impossible to be an "antifamily company," wouldn't it? So, take note that the mission statement can and should put forth principles that are hard to be against.) If your company is all about competitive pay, profit sharing, and high-quality benefits, say so, and you will draw employees who align with those principles.

After a mission statement or credo has been put forth, the principles declared within it offer guidance, especially in times of crisis. Some of you may remember the 1982 Tylenol scare that became a defining moment for Johnson & Johnson. Someone had tainted packages of extra-strength Tylenol in the Chicago, Illinois, area with huge doses of cyanide. That act killed seven people. Nearly overnight, America and the world were on alert. As a result, Tylenol dropped from a 37 percent market share to 7 percent, and the company had to determine how to quickly address the problem, restore consumer confidence, and save their reputation. Johnson & Johnson's response was *textbook* in an exemplary way, and they found guidance for their actions in their credo. Johnson & Johnson decided not to spin the story with slick corporate PR or assign blame to employees, distributors, or retailers, even though it was known that the murderer had tampered with the Tylenol *after* it was on the shelves, long out of Johnson & Johnson's control. Instead, Johnson & Johnson referred back to their credo, which initially states, that their first responsibility is to "doctors, nurses and patients, to mothers and fathers."

With that as guidance, they put a national recall in place, retrieving and destroying 31 million bottles of Tylenol at a reported loss of more than $100 million dollars. Advertising campaigns for the product were pulled, and new advertising was prepared. The product was returned to the shelves only after a triple-layered tamper-proof cap system was invented. The leadership bet that stockholders would understand this adherence to principle, and that the stockholders would have faith that the brand would emerge stronger for their conscientious action. And they bet correctly. Johnson & Johnson's response to the crisis is now the subject of studies at the university post-graduate level. It was exemplary behavior, and it was enabled, in strong part, by the existence of a sincere credo, and the fact that the credo described a corporate culture that truly believed, *and behaved*, in alignment with those principles. How much easier it must have been for Johnson & Johnson employees to confirm their links to the company and its mission after such a selfless and exemplary performance. "They really care about people more than money! I'm people—they care about me! It makes sense for me to make the effort to make them successful, and I can always be proud of my relationship with them, in my community and with my family and friends."

Now you may be thinking I am taking the easy way out by referring to pharmaceutical companies' mission statements. After all, those companies are in the business of making people healthy, and it would be hard to disagree with that as a guiding principle for any business. The real test would be for a company that makes something that doesn't necessarily make people healthy. Like furniture, for example.

Take a look at the mission statement for the office furniture maker Herman Miller. "Herman Miller, Inc., is a leading global provider of office furniture and services that create great places to live, learn, work and heal." Just as we saw with the pharmaceutical companies, this mission statement declares the company's principles in a way that broadcasts the Herman Miller culture to prospective employees (and customers!). If you don't have the temperament, or patience, or level of conscientiousness to work at a place whose mission it is to create "great places to live, learn, work and heal," then you should look elsewhere for work, because there is little chance that you will align with the company. However, if reading that mission statement inspires you, makes your heart flutter a little, and you can imagine a future in service of those goals, then there is a good chance that you will align with this corporate culture. When employees are asked what they do for a living working at Herman Miller, they may choose to respond that they design furniture or source fabric, but I bet a fair number of them say something like, "I help build great places to work."

Are your employees so aligned that they would say something similar, something in alignment with the aspirations declared in the mission of your operation? They had better be able to do so, because they are your ambassadors at home, in their communities, in their churches, and among *prospective employees* they meet in their social interactions. In fact, I can think of few more effective recruiting techniques for high-quality people than the "recruits" that come to your company because they have witnessed an employee talking with pride about his work outside the workplace. As a "recruit" looks upon the proud employee, the recruit may not say, "Hey, I want to design and sell chairs." But she may wistfully say, "Well, whatever that guy does, *that's* the way I want to feel about my workplace." That's alignment.

Now that you know the importance of a mission statement and the role it plays in alignment, you have to look at how to bring your organization's culture in alignment with the statement, and vice versa. In other words, you are reading this and saying, "That's fine for Johnson & Johnson and Merck and Hermann Miller, with all their resources and HR fire power, but how do I do this in my shop, today?

Often it's just a matter of simply and publicly stating your goal. Many people refer to this as the *BHAG—Big Hairy Audacious Goal*, as popularized by Jim Collins's book *Built to Last*. A BHAG is important, because you need a statement that people can get excited about, that people can rally around. In a tandem effort, it's often good to also identify an enemy that is important to defeat. That enemy can be a competitor, or it can be an abstract principle such as mediocrity, poverty, or cynicism. Once you start down this path, with a little bit of vision and *great deal* of discipline, dedication, honesty, and transparency—and no playing people politics, you are fully a meritocracy now!—you can reach out to your current workforce, and the workforce you intend to hire, to "literalize" the goals, to describe activities, projects, and processes that deliver on the mission statement. These activities, projects, and processes have to make sense on a practical level to the employee, but they also must be seen in the light of and in the context of how they contribute to the BHAG. This isn't something you can do in a day, or in six months. It is a continual process, where you announce your mission and stick by it as demonstrated by your actions. The employee will be the ultimate judge, and it will be evident whether the employees are with you as you all try to push the rock up the hill.

In an earlier example I cited a phrase used when the Four Seasons hotels train new employees. They state that Four Seasons employees are "ladies and gentlemen serving ladies and gentleman." I refer back to that, because it fits so well as a summary example of the points I am trying to get across here.

Just as with Merck, Johnson & Johnson, and Hermann Miller, this Four Seasons credo can be referred to for guidance for corporate behavior, for personal behavior, and to determine *personal alignment* even for people who don't yet work for Four Seasons. The truly engaged employees (or hopeful prospects) feel as though they can live by that guiding principle and enter the workplace every day with this statement guiding their personal and professional behavior.

What I suggest in this rule is as essential as it is demanding to execute. But the initial implementation is likely the hardest aspect of creating a mission-statement-directed company. As with these larger more seasoned companies, the principles take on a life of their own, as more and more of your organization's activities and procedures are driven to align with and work in harmony with your BHAG desires.

I do some consulting work with an emerging U.K. company, Red Gate, Ltd, a software company that competes in the competitive data base software marketplace. The co-CEOs Neil Davidson and Simon Galbraith take the topic of alignment seriously. They are convinced that the "manifesto" that they have published and communicated to their employees is a fair and comprehensive representation of the values and long-term goals of the company, and (they hope) for the managers and employees. But merely to post the document and to reinforce it was not enough ("to say it is so, does not make it so"). Neil and Simon called on the head of HR, Hannah Whatling, to build a platform for alignment between employee and company aspirations. What Hannah has done is not so much unique in its formation as it is in the way it was strategized and how it is being executed.

She had Red Gate join a consortium of mostly Cambridge, U.K.-based companies that built a collective people- and management-development incubator. The incubator enlisted public and private training and education providers to serve as sources for the learning and growth interests of Red Gate staffers. To enlighten and entertain, the incubator has also engaged speakers and lecturers on various topics, and most importantly they have provided resources, including money and time, to make the experiences readily available to employees. The training and education are not presented as punishment or as an R&R day-off-site reward. It really is focused personal development and career training. With this approach, Red Gate is building a "learning organization" from the inside out, and the company continues to use and assign specific training elements to bridge knowledge-and-skill gaps. But Red Gate also uses the consortium participation as a platform for employees to meet personal learning and career goals. The fact that employees who participate are more likely to achieve at a higher level of contribution is not lost on the leaders. But whoever said that sensitivity to issues that drive employees, alignment, and external focus are less worthy of merit, just because they originated out of the enlightened self-interest of the organization?

12

Understand Human Capital

There is a widely held notion among many leaders and managers, and particularly in the domains of CFOs, that "human capital" is "the employees," the physical presence of those people who companies recruit, hire, and pay. Sorry, but that's wrong! It couldn't be more wrong, and the mind-set that breeds that misconception is at the root of what troubles many organizations today. Executives and managers who want to be great leaders, and organizations that want to be great organizations, must understand what human capital is and develop the tools and skills to leverage it.

So then, what is human capital? It is the *application* of "everything about an employee" to the purposes that contribute to an organization's success. That's a little vague, I realize, so let me clarify. When I say "everything about an employee," I want you to understand my use of that word "everything" by referring to earlier rules discussed in this book, including all we have said about engagement, alignment, the employee's acculturation, the illusive discretionary effort we so eagerly want to coax forth, and the collaborative (nontoxic!) community workplace spirit that must exist in every organizational setting.

Before I get into specifics and cite examples, let me make another broad comment: Human capital can also be understood as the wealth-generating potential that exists within the people who work for an organization, and it embraces all facets of their knowledge, skills, and intellectual properties; it encompasses the skills, experiences, *and effort* of your workforce. It is their ability (and their willingness) to do things on behalf of the enterprise.

That said, when I hear people say that human capital is "the people," it doesn't exactly boil my blood, but it makes it hot enough to make tea. Calling human capital " the people" puts you into the mindset that people and their "output" can be expressed and managed solely with numerical terms. It assumes that productivity can be understood only by how much someone produces over a certain period of time. It supports the notion that time-and-motion studies accurately measure effort and productivity.

If you are thinking to yourself that what I just described is "just the way it is," or maybe *"the way it should be"* I want you to put the book down. Now! You can't be saved....

Why? Because that's Theory X Management all over again.

Remember, Theory X Management assumes people need to be managed, pushed, and supervised. It assumes that they won't produce unless you threaten to take something away from them or lure them with tangible incentives. From Theory X Management, it's a surprisingly short and easy leap to managing people punitively. But I can assure you that with a Theory X approach, after you have maybe achieved a few productivity "sugar highs," over time, your turnover will spike, as will your talent acquisition costs, and your long-term productivity will drop dramatically. Guaranteed.

If you have been following the arguments I have made so far in this book, you will recognize that there is a real risk for organizations that do not understand human capital or that manage and treat people poorly. If the organization thinks that human capital is just employee head counts and per capita output—and doesn't see that it's not just employees but what they can do when *nurtured* and *optimized* as engaged individuals—then human capital management is taken *from* the human resources office and *ceded to* the financial analysts, the cold-hearted numbers guys (and I say that with all due affection). When people become numbers on a spreadsheet, they are no longer "at the table"; they are "on the menu."

How did financial analytics become the dominant mode of management in many organizations today? It's probably not a surprise to you that people were seen as output and production machines when the industrial revolution mind-set initially took hold. But how has this concept lingered for so long through supposedly enlightened times? Well, one root cause of the problem is that academia and institutions began looking at workplaces through the use of analytic and empirical terms, especially when measuring productivity. These efforts were aimed at quantifying various aspects of workplace behavior and tying it to metrics-based value appraisals. Fair enough; it brought validity to the work and probably made it easier to publish results in peer-review journals. But the capacity for human output got subsequently confused with the understanding of human assets. They were erroneously perceived as one and the same thing.

Today, progressive, insightful human resources experts (and I like to put myself in that category) have had to work hard to discourage organizations and management from looking at people as nothing more than interchangeable parts. We have made an effort to show that people are just as valuable to organizations as the buildings and the equipment that the organization owns, maintains, and invests in. In short, organizations need to see their people as investments, and each one individually unique.

Today, we are not at a point where organizations—even forward-thinking organizations—put people on their balance sheets as fixed assets. (Of course, that doesn't mean you shouldn't treat them that way and invest in them the way you invest in other fixed assets. More on that later in this rule.) So, the problem for organizations of all sizes is that if you continue to wrongly categorize human capital, and you don't treat it as an asset, then you run the risk of missing the opportunity to maximize and leverage the available human capital to achieve enduring and sustainable success of your organization. You miss the opportunity to have people contribute at the highest level, in part because you can't appropriately communicate and demonstrate to them that they are valuable and important! Think about it: If you see your people only as numbers on a balance sheet, as interchangeable parts with no particular individual value, how can you possibly communicate to them that they are individual and unique? It is apples and oranges forever. On the other hand, if you recognize each employee's individual value, you can make the proper investment to better train the individual, to offer better guidance, to offer specific objectives and deliverables. In short, you open yourself to the opportunity to maximize your employees' ability to be successful and make you successful.

Let me take this a little further. A leader or manager has to understand how human capital works, because only then can she create an effective communication strategy to convey that value to the employee, *on an individual basis*. Often in this book I have pointed out that people want to be a part of something; they want to contribute. I have also put equal weight on the importance of letting the employee know the role he plays in creating value for the overall organization.

To optimize an employee's talent and truly engage him, the employee has to see where his daily activity is an asset to the company and a value to himself. Think about this on a human level. If you are great at your job, and you know you are great at your job, it's nonetheless demoralizing to have your work go unrecognized; it's disheartening to not be able to see where your superb work contributes on a grand scale, or, worst of all, to have the work dismissed, even out of benign negligence, as a nonasset to the organization. I can tell you story after story about star players—A-list star performers who you would pay a fortune to have on your team—simply walking away from a job because they didn't see their overall value in the larger picture. Money can't take the place of this recognition of value. It has to come person to person, with recognition that the "human output machine" is really a valuable individual worthy of respect, investment, and recognition. That's something a paycheck or a bonus can never do. And it is certainly something a spreadsheet cannot ever do; it's something only insightful leaders and managers can do.

When you look at human capital and human assets as separate things, it changes the whole game to your competitive advantage. After all, assets are defined as tangible or intangible, and they have been obtained (or are owned by) an organization for any of three general reasons. First, they promise a future benefit or hold the prospect of having a positive impact on revenues. Second, the organization "controls the asset" (maybe "locks up" is a better phrase), because the competition isn't using the asset to gain a competitive advantage. And third, when you hire someone, you are really obtaining the rights to their human capital, and you don't have to expend energy to obtain those rights over and over again. You engage in one deal (the act of hiring), and you control that asset until the employee leaves.

With these three asset characteristics in mind, let's look at how they can change the value proposition for organizations. For instance, instead of looking at human capital as a cost center to be managed for savings (the way you manage and allocate, say, physical inventory), you start to think of human capital as an asset to be developed, maintained, and invested in. And you do this with the same eye toward long-term saving that you bring to investment in other assets, such as buildings, Internet servers, inventory, and infrastructure. Moreover, this shift in mind-set is an opportunity here for a far more profound shift in thinking to take place, as well. Leadership and managers can start to view "outlays of cash" in support of human capital development as worthwhile *investments—with a demonstrable ROI*—if the money is used to attract, retain, train, and develop the right people.

As for the demonstrable ROI, the financial guys love that, the top execs love that, the corporate boards love that, and ultimately the stockholders love it. If they *all* saw human capital as an asset to be protected, and they *all* saw the bottom-line contribution made by a consistent (as opposed to transient) workforce of engaged people, the phrase "human resource expense" might cease to exist and be replaced by the phrase "human resource investment."

Though it makes it easier on leaders and managers when boards and stockholders see cash outlays as human resource *investments*, it has a far more profound effect on the employees. They take notice. They get engaged. They start to see that management is demonstrating by its actions (and capital investment) that the individual employee is an important and essential part of the organization. Believe me, if you are transitioning to a progressive company in this respect, *just the statement* of this understanding of employee value elicits a great, collective sigh of relief from the employees. And you might even hear a few people mutter, "Well it's about time!" They see that statement as evidence that a tangible step has been taken to bring actions in alignment with the intentions expressed in the C suite.

Dr. Jim Goodnight, the cofounder of SAS Institute, used to say, "If you treat people as though they make a difference, they will make a difference." He certainly made his bet on the side of the employees at SAS, and he put SAS in the position to generate wealth and competitive advantage by viewing his employees as assets, and putting the capital resources—no small investment, indeed!—toward creating a world-class people-focused infrastructure. And talk about ROI and buy-in across every department! It's hard to argue with the success, and SAS's experience of a 3 percent turnover rate in a high-salary sector where 20 percent turnover was the norm. When you are putting up numbers like that, you start to win over even those CFO types who look down their glasses like someone out of a Dickens novel, questioning every penny.

Mike Croxson is the chief operating officer and president of Ascend One, a multifaceted financial services company on the East Coast. He and his executive team have built a model of performance management that gets to the heart of leveraging human capital for the benefit of both employee and company. In a straightforward process, employees are asked to do an analysis of what they are good at doing, what they like to do, and what the company expects them to accomplish. After that, Mike makes no high-minded speeches about what it takes for leaders to leverage human capital. He has a fundamental belief that great leaders are men and women who recognize that it is the people (and what they are willing as well as able to do) that determine whether the enterprise, large or small, is going to accomplish its goal.

He says that good leaders know what needs to happen, can communicate the opportunities and impediments, and can get the people engaged in completing tasks, meeting objectives, and solving problems. The real trick is getting human capital in motion and aimed at the business result. That has nothing to do with being charismatic. The kind of leadership that leverages human capital is the leadership that can articulate a challenge or goal, show the worthiness of the goal, and the win-win possibility of achieving the goal—and then rallying people around the execution of tasks that bring the desired results.

That's it! From Mike's perspective, you simply have to understand what the need is and why it is important to have it satisfied. You have to communicate the value of the desired result, and how it brings those business and personal wins with it. You have to show confidence in the skills, aptitudes, and attitudes of those you entrust with executing the tasks. And you must provide appropriate resources. That kind of leadership and that management style gets the human capital engine humming.

Now, Mike does say that sometimes leaders can be successful leveraging human capital by merely setting things in motion toward a goal. He characterizes that as "giving the time of day" without feeling the need to explain "how a watch is built." But, he notes that in some cases, particularly when working to engage employees truly is a new way of doing things, it is essential for the leader to explain enough about the inner works of the watch to get people believing that you are giving them the correct time. In cases where the trust is shaky or the "people-centric" approach to strategy and tactics is new, the role that leadership plays and the behavior of the leader is critical. As

Mike Croxson describes it in his soft drawl, "You've got to foster principled leadership to get the best out of people. Not the most—the best!" He defines Ascend One's "principled leadership" as a pattern of behaving in ways that foster two-way trust and respect, while focusing on results, driving hard for business performance, and developing talent. "You can't have leaders who go around saluting the flag, while kickin' the dog," he says without the hint of a smile.

When making the effort to tap into the human capital of employees, executives and managers sometimes make the error of trying to lift the level of contribution of average or below average performers, instead of creating an environment that unleashes the full human capital of the outstanding contributors. This error is often committed for the best of reasons: Leadership's obligation is to develop its people. But to spend 60 percent to 80 percent of one's nurturing time on the 20 percent of people who may have the least human capital to contribute, all the while putting the attention and enthusiasm of high potential employees at risk, is poor management and faulty leadership.

The next question we ask about human capital is this: How do leaders determine the value of human capital? When you walk the halls of many American offices, there are these posters *ad nauseam* about Teamwork and Loyalty and Effort. These are the posters you see for sale in the in-flight magazines; you know the ones I am talking about. Almost all of them state in some way the belief that "people are our greatest asset." First of all, saying so doesn't make it so, and more importantly—at the end of the day—individuals are not assets. They are volunteers. I have said elsewhere in this book that 90 percent of your assets walk out the door everyday, and maybe—if you treat them well, give them meaningful work, and communicate their value—they come back the next day, eager to contribute even more.

Inspiring employees to come back each day, and inspiring them to contribute, is the result of an increasingly sophisticated field of HR called *talent management*. Talent management recognizes at its core that an asset is worth more than the cost to acquire it, and at the core of talent management is the driving need to develop and nurture your organization's human assets, to present individuals with interesting career paths, to offer them ways and means to expand their horizons, to avail them of educational and growth opportunities. It's a method of partnering with your employees so that they grow and actualize, and the organization benefits by the growth.

All of what I have covered in this rule is really in broad recognition that employees deliver when they are engaged, when they are aligned, and when they feel as though they are valued—and contributing something of value in return. When you build corporate engagement structures, all of the employees' future activity—the expanding talents and abilities of your human assets—becomes integral to a process that creates cash flow. And don't get me wrong, at the end of the day, it's that cash that makes all this possible.

13

Treat Employees as "Volunteers"

Although we, as the executors of business strategy and expert tacticians, find and hire the talented people at all levels who perform the tasks that move the wheels of our companies forward, we are really not as much in control of our "human assets," as we once were. You see, we are the buyers, and it is no longer a buyer's market when it comes to talent acquisition.

Generational differences, attitudes toward loyalty, and the reality that employees have no reasonable expectation of career-long employment with one (or even two) companies, are just three of the factors that contribute to making this a seller's market. That said, the biggest factor is the simple but undeniable law of supply and demand.

So I want to revisit the persistent (and wrong) notion that there are consistently more job seekers available than there are jobs to be filled.

A couple of decades ago, 1987 to be exact, the Hudson Institute published an influential study called *Workforce 2000*. It was updated in 1997 as *Workforce 2020*. The reports are heralded as a wake-up call to employers in the United States, because they clearly state that the supply of skilled and talented workers is shrinking year after year and will continue to do so until the middle of this century. In 2000, there were more high-tech, high-knowledge, high-touch jobs than there were people to fill them, and that trend continues today. Key jobs in many companies go begging, and the average **time to fill rate** (a metric used by HR and staffing professionals to measure how long a job stays open from the time it is first advertised till the new employee's first day of work) has stretched from two to three months to as long as one year for many professional and technical positions. Statistics from the Department of Labor projected that from 2000 to 2010 there would be a 23.7 percent rise in demand for workers with PhDs (to 353,000), and a 22.5 percent rise in demand for workers with bachelor's degrees (to 4,006,000), with no reasonable expectation that the supply of candidates would match the need.

If that does not impress you, maybe this will: 84 percent of baby boomers (people ages 44 to 62 in 2008) participate in the labor market, and those boomers make up nearly 50 percent of the 2008 workforce. But over the next 30 years, *76 million* of these baby boomers will retire, and only 46 million new workers from Generations X and Y will have entered the labor force. That's a possibility of 30 million empty job slots. And the government's current stand on legal immigration and work visas doesn't offer much hope, for sure; and neither does the growth of economies around the Pacific Rim, the Indian subcontinent, and Eastern Europe, where the United States has always found talented candidates, eager and willing to emigrate to the United States to walk the "streets of gold."

In a January 2003 survey of 3,800 employers nationwide, 51 percent of employers said they have a "hard" or "very hard" time finding qualified employees (*Rising to the Challenge*, U.S. Chamber of Commerce, 2003).

Peter Capelli of the University of Pennsylvania's Wharton School of Business, is on record as saying that the *Workforce 2000* and *Workforce 2020* reports are in error and that there is no real need to panic about whether there will be a sufficient number of talented job candidates to go around. But I, among others, disagree. My disagreement stems from my personal talks with business leaders and HR execs, and from the results of CEO surveys, which consistently list finding and keeping talented people as one of the three most prominent business issues that keep them awake at night. They know from experience that good employees are hard to find—and hard to keep.

So let me reintroduce this rule by saying that you really need to begin thinking of your employees as volunteers, and treating them as such. If you come from a mind-set that thinks the labor market is always in favor of the employer and that workers are much like modular and interchangeable parts that can be dealt with as chattel, or if you think that behind one departing employee is a large group of equally valuable potential candidates lined up to take her place, I hope to persuade you otherwise.

It's true that some low-skill, repetitive-motion jobs—especially in boom-bust sectors such as construction and simple production manufacturing—are not begging for applicants. But most positions that require midlevel skills, serious education, training, problem-solving, and decision-making go begging for talent. This problem is particularly evident among the talented professional classes, or among the "creative classes," the hires who bring your organization real innovations, new products, reliable growth, and long-term relationships. Within these groups, anyone with real talent can go find a new job, more money, bigger office, "nicer" geography/climate tomorrow. No matter what the unemployment rate, whether it's 1 percent or 17 percent, there is always a market for talent.

So, what does it mean to treat employees as volunteers? Where do we find examples? Well, I suggest you look at those organizations you come into contact with nearly every day that by design are cash-flow stressed, or use their cash for purposes external to the organization itself. I am speaking of charities, or community improvement enterprises, or others cut from the same cloth. Yes, I am talking about "do-gooders."

For a number of years my father-in-law, Art, a retired auto parts salesman and WWII vet, volunteered his time every week at the large VA hospital in Durham, North Carolina. He didn't have a lot of money to contribute, so his way to give back was to volunteer at a place, and to a purpose, with which he could identify and where he felt a connection. It was also a social connection for him, and so it gave back to him and the other men and women who volunteered with him.

At the hospital, he performed a simple task—he escorted patients to doctor visits or to lab tests, by pushing or accompanying their wheelchairs to the appropriate hospital locations. His "job" was to get them there, and on time, and get them back. No title, no pay, no problem!

Art hardly ever missed a volunteer day, and he was usually early. On days when he was scheduled to work, he turned down offers from me and other friends for lunches or day trips to museums, because the hospital needed him. I knew that he was performing a service for the VA, one that helped reduce the need for additional paid staff, but until the day I attended a volunteer luncheon with Art and my wife, I didn't really understand the full measure of his dedication to his service.

The luncheon was a simple affair with no cloth napkins or gourmet foods, but it was special, really special. All the heads of hospital administration were there, and a few of the doctors attended. Those busy and important people spent the majority of the 90 minutes giving out awards for attendance, or friendliness, or whatever. But more importantly the officials from the VA spent the time telling the volunteers how special they were, and how important their service was to the facility and to the patients. The volunteers were given lavish praise for their consistency and their loyalty, and were told that they counted, that their input and suggestions were important, and that they made the world of that VA hospital a better one.

Art and his fellow volunteers beamed, although slightly embarrassed by the attention and said privately afterward that they were honored to be associated with that institution. They wanted to be there to continue to render service. For free!

Why? Each of them could be otherwise occupied, tending a garden, playing golf, reading books, or doing any number of satisfying and enjoyable things to pass retirement hours. But they chose to go back to volunteering again and again, because the staff made it a priority to make them feel wanted, needed, and valuable. The administration showed respect for the volunteers, their service, their input and ideas, treating them like precious cargo, rather than an unimportant business necessity.

So the challenge for leaders becomes to get their own employees to want to come back to work each week, to want to boost the competitive advantages of the employer, to want to contribute at the highest level possible for the tasks assigned. And since the shortest distance between two points is still a straight line, you can meet that challenge by treating employees as though they are volunteers—by behaving as though you really need them to show up again tomorrow and by acknowledging that they do have choices. If you have hired the right people, as long as they choose you, you can win.

And now for an Andy Rooney moment: *Have you ever noticed…*that in times of stress or economic turmoil or market downturns, the best companies grow and even thrive, increasing the size of the gap between themselves and their competitors? Have you ever wondered how they do it? It's largely because they have the best people. The dedication of those people to the success of their employers is the difference—the secret sauce.

Now, if the scenarios presented to us by *Workforce 2000* and *Workforce 2020* play out, job seekers will recognize that the playing field tilts in their favor, and they will feel it, see it, and know it before the staffing administrators within corporations have the first clue. Then the job seekers will look for jobs within companies that treat employees "right." Those people-centric employers will pick from the best-suited candidates and move on. The rest of the pack of employers will be left to fight over the rejected many.

It's not only wrong to make rash assumptions about supposedly endless pools of talent, it's expensive to do so as well. In other rules discussed in this book, I have cited the consensus estimation of the cost of recruiting and training a replacement employee—the costs of voluntary turnover. (Oh, let's call it what it is: *defection!*) For professionals and managers, it's upwards of 150 percent of their salaries. So, as you march some unwanted fellow off the plank and think that you can bring on another ready shipmate eager to take his place, get out your checkbook, because you're going to need it. You'll be writing checks until you go broke.

Another widely circulated employer-employee workplace dynamic (except this one is true!) is that cradle-to-the-grave employment is long gone. It's been destroyed by decades of plant closings, mergers and acquisitions, and the exportation of jobs to cheaper overseas labor markets. That's not news. But what might be news to you now is that this dynamic has changed *both* sides of the employment equation. Understanding this cultural shift is crucial to the points I make in this rule. The fact is today's workers don't expect long-term employment. As ideal it may have been to work 25 years for Big Blue or Ma Bell and retire with a lake house and an irrevocable pension package, it just doesn't happen that way any more. That has changed the way the employer looks at the employee. But here's the key: It has also changed the way the employee looks at the employer.

These days, employees operate in what is essentially a barter economy. The employees, particularly Gen X, Gen Y, and the newest kids on the block, offer to barter their skills and give themselves wholly over to an employer in exchange for fair pay, benefits, and opportunities for professional growth. These employees come to work, and they see each day as an opportunity to provide intellectual capital, hard work, and services. In exchange for that, they want fair pay and ample fringe benefits, advancement, and the ability to learn and grow. This differs substantially from decades past. In those days, the baby boomer went to the pay window, accepted his pay, and said to the employer "Thanks for the opportunity to work here." But the new generation of workers, the one in barter economy mode, goes to the pay window, accepts the check, looks the paymaster straight in the eye and says, "We're even. I believe I'll see you Monday."

Employees are far more willing to consider other work options, *all the time*. They are willing to risk their skills and aptitudes in the marketplace, including the skills that their current employer paid them to learn! In this barter relationship, anything—especially any violation of trust or fairness, any hint of a plantation mentality on the part of management that breaks the barter bond between the employer and the employee—is justification for the employee to seek work elsewhere at the drop of a hat, and at the aforementioned enormous cost to the employer.

The twenty-first century employee doesn't feel beholden to the organization. She knows that, even after all the kind words and encouragement, if the board and the CFO say, "We are going to cut the entire division to save costs," the employee is gone. And no kind words or good relationships with a local manager are going to change that. On the other hand, the employee reads the same media reports and books that managers read, and she, too, is acutely aware of the labor market. She also knows the prohibitive cost of finding, hiring, and onboarding replacement workers for the employer. So, she calculates that into her value, as well.

So, with today's workplace culture and the forever-changed nature of the employee-employer dynamic, it is essential for employers to recognize that employees are volunteers. They volunteer to work for you and vote, sometimes daily, whether to show up for work. If the relationship between the employee and the employer is productive for both sides of the equation, the employer sees the value of keeping that employee on board, while always calculating the cost of a replacement. And the employee is constantly looking for the demonstration of continued commitment by the employer to his growth, and to his overall value. Any employer who intends to profit in the barter economy (or at least not incur unreasonable labor costs) must recognize why employees stay, and the employer must nurture employees with a special focus on these "sweet spots."

Why do they stay? I've said it elsewhere, and I'll say it again. Employees stay if they love what they do; if they have positive social relationships at the workplace; if they have a good relationship with bosses. Overall, they stay if they are *engaged*, and I use the word engaged to encompass, in a summary way, everything I have detailed in this book, such as the alignment of the employee's personal concerns and the company's concerns; a sense of trust, transparency, honesty, and respect in the workplace. If one or more of these things is missing, breaks down, or is taken away, the bond is loosened and at risk, and strains of "Take This Job and Shove It" become the background music of all thoughts about work. And sooner or later your "talent" is on the way down the street to work for your competitor.

For people-intensive companies, about 90 percent of your assets walk out the door every day. (For machine-driven or real-estate dominated companies, your people asset percentage may be as low as 40 percent to 50 percent.) But, regardless, people are the repositories of institutional knowledge and intellectual capital. I have seen that truism play out at every place I have worked, and especially with my nearly two decades at SAS Institute. In fact, in the late 1980s, after I had been at SAS for the better part of a decade, a local newspaper sent a reporter to talk with me. He had heard about all the people-focused and family-friendly policies we had at SAS. In the course of our discussions, he posed this question: "Do you think it is necessary to have all these programs to get people to come to work for you?" I told him that Dr. Goodnight and I had had a brief but revealing talk early in the meteoric growth curve of the company to determine what kind of place he would build and be remembered for. His request, no, his *mandate* was a simple one: "Let's make this a place where coming to work every day is as meaningful, challenging, and as much fun for the employees as it is for the owners!" That statement harkened back to a desire that Dr. Goodnight had expressed to me when I first started working at SAS when there were just a few dozen employees. He said that he wanted the people who worked there "to feel like owners." As humanistic as these intentions were—and they have had a marked and positive impact on the lives of thousands of families—it was in the end a financial boon to implement these philosophies at SAS. That's because if the people who left each day decided not to come in the follow day, we were toast. We would have no competitive advantage, and the company would have collapsed. That's not an exaggeration. We knew it, and the employees knew it. The employees were bartering their services with a highly eager and motivated partner.

Don't get me wrong. The reason for building a great people-focused infrastructure at SAS came authentically from the heart, and these policies have always expressed the sincere and best intentions of the leadership. That said, the philosophy of caring for people was coupled with the enlightened business self-interest that also compelled us to engage employees in this way. And it paid off. The results of the policies, programs, and behaviors were easy to see. Our employee base—which grew to nearly 7,000 before I retired—developed a psychological ownership of the company, and of the software and services the company produced. They also took ownership of the customer relationships and engaged our customers and products on every level as owners would.

What inspired them to do this? It's really rather simple. Their response was typically human. We treated them fairly, as adults, with respect, and as volunteers. They responded fairly, as adults, acting with respect, and...as *volunteers*. In multiple areas of their work and family life, we inspired them to wake up each day and say, "I'm going to go to work today and do a great job for someone who respects me, helps me take care of my family, and treats me well. I can't see any reason to move on...so far." The spirit of employee engagement at SAS was extraordinary, and extra effort, the kind of effort you see from volunteers, was a relatively common feature of our workplaces, globally.

Yet, like any wise person who won't be played the fool, the employees were always watchful of anything that would break the barter bond

I alluded to earlier. And they were always aware (but not defensive), because they knew that they were gaining increasingly valuable skills as they grew in their professional development at SAS. Given the demographics for people in their practice areas (software development) many of them knew that they had highly marketable skills. So we continually responded, and our response resonated with them. And it continues to do so today. Year after year the employee turnover rate at SAS is around *17 percent below* the industry norm, and that turnover difference saves SAS millions of hard dollars each year.

So, my advice to you is this: Heed the warnings of the Hudson Institute; pay attention to the management behaviors of the enterprises that cultivate volunteer workers; and learn from the world's most noted people-focused workplaces. Finally, teach your executives, particularly your CFO, to regard resources spent on attracting and retaining talent as investments rather than expenses. The returns are phenomenal.

14

Know Your Culture

Pop quiz. And no cheating, okay? *Promise?*

Without stopping to think, can you succinctly explain your organization's culture? If you were put in front of a room of new employees, or even a roomful of legacy employees, could you articulate your culture and list your organization's aspirations? Could you conduct a briefing on how your company came to be as it is today, how it thinks, feels, and behaves, and what your culture means for the human resources and marketing departments, so that they can subsequently communicate and brand it, externally and internally?

If you can do this (and I hope you can, because even if your culture isn't all you hope for, you still have to know it to change it), ask yourself this: Can your *employees* do the same? Can you sit three or four "average" employees in a room and—without coaching and with no preparation—and ask them to describe in a sentence or two your organization's core culture? You know, can they give "the elevator speech"—the one that can inform a total stranger about the who, what, when, where, and how of your organization?

How about your managers? How about your vice presidents?

Now, take the discussion outside the company. Do your long-term suppliers and contractors know your culture? And, oh, don't forget about all the customers. Do you think your *customers* can describe what your company is all about? It follows logically that if you don't know your culture, there's little chance your employees, suppliers, and customers will guess it correctly when asked, and that doesn't speak well of the future prospects of your organization.

Whether you are selling replacement parts for $1 flashlights or high-fidelity supply chain optimization software that costs millions of dollars a copy, culture is undeniably essential to employee recruiting and retention, vendor relationships, customer loyalty, long-term success, and overall company value.

Now here's the second part of the pop quiz. Can you tell stories—even stories that rise to the level of the mythical—about the history of your organization and its successes? By "myth," I mean stories that retell the tale of an effort that was exemplary, stories that metaphorically represent the organization's mission, aspirations, personality, and style. Maybe these stories describe something big and bold, as when your organization triumphed over adversarial circumstances, hard times. Maybe these stories describe events that tested the wills of your leaders, employees, and/or teams to produce and deliver. Or maybe these stories describe something remarkably simple, as when a member of senior management was gracious, generous, thoughtful, humorous, or even humble, when he didn't have to be. Can you do that, off the cuff? And deliver the message with a conversational style that doesn't look as though it was just cooked up by an intern writing for your corporate communications department?

The reason I ask these "pop quiz" questions is this: Knowing your company's culture is a foundational requirement for fostering engaged employees, and a highly refined and carefully nurtured corporate culture is a bedrock element on which employee engagement is built. That said, I hope you are "two for two" on the questions that opened this rule. If not, don't sweat it, because you have had many chances for extra credit in other places in the book. So don't throw in the towel.

I recognize that you might have heard someone say, "Who has the time to give a damn about culture?" It's something I hear often as well. In fact, many managers and leaders say that they are too focused on the important stuff like *growth*, *competitiveness*, and *shareholder value* to slow down and indulge the "soft science" of nurturing employ-ees, right? They think that progressive culture and people-focused policies are luxuries reserved for companies only after they have grown rich and successful. After all, isn't the road to success littered with rust-ing hulks of companies that didn't keep their eye on the ball and got distracted from productivity, profitability, and market share by paying attention to "people issues," when they should have been focused on getting every last ounce of productivity out of employees at every level. Aren't the companies that have failed the ones who spent too much thought, time, and money on M&Ms, free food, and fitness centers, while dulling their cutting edge in the marketplace? Well?

Although I have a great deal of empathy with the organizational leaders who are eager for productivity and to see its impact on the bottom line, there are ways to engage employees and drive up pro-ductivity that have nothing to do with adversarial workplaces focused on punitive organizational dynamics, and "killer instinct." In fact, I hate to be the first one to break it to you (though I am sure that I am not), but study after study shows that companies with engaged work-forces—those supposedly "distracted" companies that take the time and dedicate the resources to optimize the productivity of their employee base through engagement, not imprisonment—are the companies that are consistently more productive and more competi-tive, with better product development, faster time-to-market, lower rates of turnover (a *dramatic* cost saver), faster stock appreciation, and greater market share. Time after time this turns out to be true. You can look it up, as Casey Stengel used to say.

It seems to me that the managers who *don't* recognize the value of a culture of engagement are the ones who shareholders and boards of directors should hold suspect. Given the research—and there is plenty of it at every level, for every type and every size of company— the misfeasance practiced in the C suite these days is more likely to occur when leaders follow conventional wisdom like so many lem-mings to implement "strategies" that work *against* high employee retention, strong growth, higher stock values, and competitive advantage by *ignoring* culture. You can't grow long-term value by believing that the best way to build a company is to play the autocrat, the dictator, the low-balling, slash-and-burn bargain hunter with no vision beyond the quarterly balance sheet that shows short-term growth at any cost, human or otherwise.

Let's take a closer look at exactly how culture shows itself, and how you can build an infrastructure to let a great culture emerge.

What Makes a Great Work Culture?

A couple of years ago, I went to the wedding of a daughter of a dear friend of mine. My friend is an executive at John Deere, and though he had been lured away from John Deere to join another company for a brief period, he had recently returned to the company. He had moved his family back to the Quad Cities area of Illinois and Iowa, where John Deere is headquartered, to accept a promotion to the home office.

As part of the wedding festivities, the out-of-town wedding guests were invited to the rehearsal dinner. Where was the dinner held? *At the John Deere Historic Site, in the exhibit hall.* Oh sure, it was decked out for fancy dining with sumptuous foods, linen tablecloths, and silver place settings. There was great service and fabulous wines. But what amazed me was the fact that the family, including the bride—with more than a few options for opulent dining surrounding the events leading up to the young lady's wedding—would choose to have the dinner among displays of new and vintage farm machinery! What was even more remarkable was the high level of camaraderie I witnessed among my friend's coworkers, many who were also guests at the dinner. They were all enormously proud to show off the company's products and talk about the history of the machinery and the company. No one was ashamed of the greatness of John Deere or its impact on the exec and his family, or their individual and group relationships with the equipment giant, even though we all could have been at a nearby country club or elegant restaurant. During the evening—remember, I was there for his elder daughter's prewedding festivities—we guests got tours of the huge harvesters and combines, and we got to look at the air conditioning systems, the stereos, and all the bells and whistles. It was a terrific night for all and quite eye opening! But honestly, how many of *your* employees would choose to have a daughter's rehearsal dinner reception in a hall on your corporation's or organization's campus where the products you produced were on display? How many would opt for drinks at a country club instead of a tour of the latest services or gear coming off your production lines? In a word, the scene I just described shows that the employees at John Deere are *truly engaged*. The community of people created at work extends beyond the work environment and into their personal lives. They were full of pride for what they produced and for the company that employed them.

Now, do you think they are productive during their workday, too? *You bet.*

Think they go the extra mile to make a good product great? *You win again!*

Think they stay the extra hours and exert that "discretionary effort" that is so illusive to the vast majority of organizations and companies? Well, I think you know the answer to that.

So, back to our pop quiz. Do you think everyone, from the leadership to the production line employees at John Deere—even to the families of those employees—could articulate John Deere's culture? How about new employees? Do new employees go through an onboarding process and come out the other end with a firm sense of what their jobs are, where they fit in, *and* the level of excellence expected of them?

More importantly, if a department or division of John Deere goes off track for some reason and needs to be righted, do you think you would have to look very far for cultural and corporate guidance to direct remedial action. And remember when I spoke of those stories that rise to the level of myth? Imagine how impressive it would be if you, like those who work at John Deere, could point out a few people in your lunch room and say, "See that guy. He thinks so much of this company and his relationship with it that he held his daughter's prewedding event right here in the company museum/showroom."

Now that's a great culture!

Another culture I admire has been implemented by George Zimmer at the Men's Wearhouse. I love going there, where I'm treated like royalty. I feel like an honored guest every single time. People remember my name, which may not seem extraordinary until you realize that the Men's Wearhouse is a discount clothing store! (How many other people at discount clothing stores that you happen upon remember your name?) I strongly suspect this culture exists because Zimmer has instilled a corporate culture where the right good people are recruited and retained, where employees are respected and therefore given "permission" through example to act with respect to coworkers and customers.

The Men's Wearhouse didn't achieve this status by putting up posters on the wall, like the "inspirational" ones you see hanging in offices across America. They didn't obtain this culture by accident. They did this through deliberate action, through diligent adherence to a set of principles, and through day-to-day activities that are always in sync with what the Men's Wearhouse wants to be. We look more closely at those strategies and other examples of great cultures in the coming pages of this book.

How Does Cuture Evolve?

If your strategy to gain competitive advantage depends on product innovations, but your innovation is stunted by a stifling organizational hierarchy and the political (as opposed to meritorious) composition of teams and departments, you have a failed strategy for establishing a winning corporate culture. If your culture rewards only superstars and A players, and treats the rest of the employees like serfs in a feudal system, you are bound to stumble. Yet corporate culture is not something that you dictate, like vacation policy and rules for expense reporting.

Some years ago, I was at a conference that featured discussions about the most-admired companies in America. During a particular presentation from a leading consulting group, which will go unnamed, I happened to be sitting next to an acquaintance of mine who then was a senior executive with Levi Strauss. The presenter started to speak about how to go about building culture. At the mention of "building culture," and the listing of the recipe ingredients, my friend and I looked at each other with our heads cocked. Then we turned back to the speaker, both sure that he had misspoken. As we listened, it turned out that "building culture" became the full *theme* of the presentation, and my friend and I kept catching each other's eyes and looking more and more doubtful. At the time, I was in my role as vice president for human resources at SAS Institute, a job I held for 19 years, and where I am proud to say I played a part in creating a company widely recognized as one of best places to work in America for many years running. As the presentation ended, my friend and I walked toward each other and said, almost simultaneously, "These guys don't get it!" You don't build culture. Even the best management teams, with the best corporate C-suite guidance, can hope only to create a work environment and infrastructure that displays compelling values, an expected behavior pattern, and a clearly articulated mission. From that, you hope that a great culture emerges, and if it doesn't, you intervene with practices and processes aimed at redirecting and changing it.

The truth is, like it or not, you are going to have a culture in your organization. It may not be the one you want, and it may be a culture that emerges by accident or even by default. It may even surprise you that a culture has evolved that is more admirable than you at first imagined. But make no mistake. You are going to have a culture.

That culture is the sum total of the emergence of the relationships among enterprise values and mission, how your leadership behaves, how your people view and treat each other, how you are viewed from the outside, and how all those things are reflected in your products and relationships to your customers and vendors. Naturally, you can't freeze a culture in place. The culture changes and evolves, as people and events change. So it is critical for managers and leaders to engage in the pick-and-shovel work to learn what your culture is *before* you attempt to build or change it, and that activity is important for a couple of reasons. First, if your organization's leaders have no idea what culture is, in an abstract and academic sense, and no specific idea what your own culture is, it is virtually impossible to put together an action plan to affect that culture. There can be no widely understood way for people to converse, explain, and understand the culture. Worse, with no firm understanding of your culture, a well-intentioned and ambitious executive may jump in with grand plans to affect the culture. But with no direction or guidance, she may implement notions, ideas, and plans that are so countercultural as to be entirely ineffective and headed for "flavor of the month" status— after you've spent considerable resources on the exercise.

So, it is critical for managers and leaders to discover their culture and bring their aspirations for the company into sync with that culture. The aspirations don't have to be high-minded. We are not necessarily trying to implement the steps leading up to sainthood here. It can be something as simple as, "We want to be big!" But it is the culture that gets your employees to "share and care." It is the culture that acts as a guiding beacon, *per se*, for the activities at every level of the company so they are brought in sync with the company's aspirations.

Take Southwest Airlines for example. They have a remarkably consistent culture across a wide, growing, and diverse employee base. If you are an observer of that company's culture, as I am, you would recognize that they have done a great job of promulgating that culture to every level of the company, from the chief executive to the newest reservations agent. It even is displayed in the painted decoration of their aircraft, which display a red heart. What is that culture? It's to celebrate accomplishments, large and small, trust your coworkers, and be willing to risk putting yourself out there. It asks employees to display a sense of humor and help one another. It expects employees to share and believe in teamwork. It teaches that you have to be able to put other people ahead of you, so the company gets ahead. If an employee is not willing to do that, to openly display "love," then he is not right for Southwest Airlines. That person is not in sync with the company culture and will be rejected or managed out. The same can be said about cultures for other admirable companies, such as Apple, Ben and Jerry's, American Eagle Outfitters, the U.S. Olympic Committee, Minitab, Inc., and Ascend One, among others. They broadcast a consistent "homing beacon" that says, *this is how we behave; this is how we succeed.* That homing beacon implicitly asks simple questions of employees, prospective new employees, contractors, vendors, and finally customers: *Do you fit in with us? Would you be honored to do business with us...because we honor those with whom we do business. We are family. Are you part of our family too?*

Nurturing Culture

If you have unintentional culture, a culture that is has evolved without nurturing, and it is detrimental to your organization's success, you must move firmly to revise the culture. How do you change culture? First, announce loudly that you find the existing culture unacceptable and not in line with the mission and vision of the organization. Then you have to change all the behaviors within the organization that drive the unacceptable aspects of it. For example, at SAS Institute, we wanted to have a culture of inclusion. It was critical to our success because our products worked best when developed collaboratively, and a culture of inclusion was one of the ways we would attract and retain employees.

So, at SAS Institute, every policy and procedure was built around making all employees feel they had a voice and some measure of real control in the processes that ran the company. We showed that what mattered to them mattered to the senior management and owner-ship. We were careful to show these employees respect and to respect the things they cared for, whether intellectually, socially, or with their families. These shared concerns were all openly and visibly important to SAS Institute. Accordingly, we offered things like an on-campus health care, day care, and fitness. It signaled to the employees that we were concerned for their well-being and the well-being of their fami-lies. Sure, you can put a price on all these things, because, believe me, they were expensive to provide. But we were signaling to our employ-ees (and top-notch prospects whom we would love to employ and keep away from our competition) that we included everyone as equals and recognized that, at the end of the day, each of them was a volunteer whom we hoped to have back the next day for a productive day at work...because they wanted to be there.

We also heavily subsidized the cafeterias and created restaurant atmospheres. All were open to employees and their families, so the chil-dren from the day-care center could regularly come over to share lunch with mom and dad, grandma and grandpa. We served nutritionally pre-pared food, not junk food. We said we wanted to be inclusive, and the infrastructure we built demonstrated the seriousness of our intentions.

We also encouraged employees to speak up in multiple forums—some online and some in-person—where we took their opinions to heart. We signaled to everyone that we welcomed complaints and con-cerns when they were offered in the spirit of cooperatively solving prob-lems. We viewed complaints as the surfacing of issues to be considered. We didn't always satisfy requests or make changes, but we surely lis-tened carefully and always responded in a reasonable amount of time.

It sounds a little too simple—too obvious to me—to be called common sense, but if you want a culture of inclusion, senior manage-ment must actually believe in including people and their ideas. If you want a culture of respect, you must have a management team that respects each other and the employees. If you want to break down organizational politics, you actually have to censure political behavior. And you absolutely must recognize and value the dignity of every contribution, from the work of the cafeteria dishwasher, through the "steady Eddie" B players, and to the high impact A players.

Once you start to establish a culture, like the culture of inclusiveness we created at SAS Institute—which over time dramatically and consistently increased our competitiveness and built a record of remarkable employee retention—you have to take the next steps to deliver on the deal you made with the workforce. Part of that is inculcating new employees into the culture through a robust orientation period, and I don't mean having a middle manager or an HR assistant show them the insurance forms, indicate the work schedules, and lead them to the office supplies closet.

Just as implementing a culture is an activity that must be taken seriously every day, so too should the acculturation of the new employee onboarding process be taken just as seriously. The onboarding process is a socialization and inculcation experience, and it should last 90 to 180 days. Moreover, it should retrieve as much information as it imparts. *Why did you come here? Why do you think you are a fit here?* These should be common questions asked of all new employees, because the answers to those questions give you an accurate read on how your culture is perceived outside the company walls. But those same questions are just as important to ask of people who have been there three, eight, and ten years, and we asked them at SAS. *Why are you* still *here? Why have you volunteered to come back day after day all these years? What do like about being here, and what rankles you?* Those answers, too, tell you a great deal about your culture.

During these processes, I can't overemphasize the importance of the CEO's personal involvement, or the importance of her physical participation in some way during every orientation. Just her presence sends the message that *you've got the attention of a very busy person.*

You're important and worth my time. We're glad you're here. It also sends the message that we honor the people we value, and here's what you can expect from your relationship with this company.

Now it goes without saying that it is crucial to have the right people at every tier in your organization, no matter how they are welcomed in the onboarding process. As Jim Collins famously says in his books *Good to Great* and *Built to Last*, it's not just good people, it's the *right* good people that matter for success and competitive advantage. Sure, you need to hire people with baseline talents and skills. But moreover you need people who can both take advantage of and complement the culture you have established, so that they can grow to be better than they were on their first day of work. That means creating a culture that offers opportunity and growth potential, and in other rules we look closely at how to align the organization's interests with the personal interests of the employee.

Additionally, you have to find people who fit. You can have the most dynamic onboarding process in the world, and you can have the CEO buying breakfasts for the five-year anniversary of an employee and giving him a one-on-one for an hour to talk about the company. You can offer free on-campus health and dental, free day care, a 40,000 square foot fitness complex, but if the skilled and prepared employee doesn't care much about the things that matter to the organization, it will all be for nothing. That's because people who don't fit, can't align. Ever. It's always a mismatch. So, your culture must serve not only as an integration tool for new employees and a guiding beacon for legacy employees, but it must also serve as a homing device for the kinds of people—the *right good people*—who are culturally in sync with the goals and aspirations of the organization.

Finally, I'd like to address the theme that I've visited throughout this book, and that's the reasons people come to work and the role culture plays here. Do you know that it's not about the money? Oh sure, you have to pay people, and pay them competitively. But the number one reason people get up and go to work isn't the money. It's that they have a visceral need to do something of worth and to contribute something of value to an entity larger than themselves—to their employer, to society, and to their own sense of self-worth. The second reason: They want to make that contribution in a place worthy of the effort and its meaning to them and their communities. They want to be proud of what they produce and benefit from how that result or outcome contributes to their relationships in life. And that pride is tied to where the contribution is made. Third, they want to leave some kind of legacy—Lee Iacocca's Mustang, Steve Jobs's Mac and iPod. Fourth, they want to do it in the company of others so that they enjoy the interaction that accompanies good work. In fact, we all talk about the importance of money, but it really is pretty far down the list. The question for the managers and leaders who are interested in culture is this: Do you have a workplace that provides an infrastructure and a context of opportunity and respect where people can contribute, be recognized for it, be proud of their production, have high levels of camaraderie, and leave a legacy—all in service of the company's growth, aspirations, success mission, and profitability? Oh, and can they do that while still wanting to proudly have their daughter's wedding reception in the company museum?

15

Understand the Nature of Change and Prepare Your Employees to Embrace It

By and large, organizations have historically displayed an unwillingness to implement necessary and productive changes to the ways they conduct business. Even when some change is introduced, most organizations fail to incorporate the change to the depth and breadth necessary to engage employees. One of the reasons for this unwillingness is old-fashioned human nature. Almost universally, organizations believe that people hate change and resist it under even the most favorable circumstances. However, people do support change (and even become early-adopters of it) *under certain conditions.* To understand why I have added *under certain conditions,* this rule shows you how to use people's natural response to change to your competitive advantage.

To understand people's reaction to change on a personal basis, you don't have to look much further than your own computer. When you get that new software upgrade from Microsoft or wherever, isn't it a pain in the neck to adjust to the change? Or I should say, isn't it a pain in the neck to be *forced to adjust* to the change? It seems as though no sooner than you have mastered the old version of the software—where you knew all the shortcuts and commands—some wise guy at the software company decides to change it on you! The software manufacturers believe they are making their product dramatically better, but you complain long and loud that you were more productive with the older version. The truth is, I'd bet you said this same thing when you were forced (depending how old you are!) to go from mainframe "green-screen" to DOS, and from DOS to Windows, and then through each of the various versions of Windows. (The jury is still out on Vista, I know!)

Let me spin out another scenario for you. Do you like golf? Or vacations? I bet you do not have the same aversion to change, to the new and different, when you try a new golf course or a new beach location. Even though it may qualify as a radical change from the pattern of your past behavior, finding the new path to the first tee doesn't seem to be a pain in the neck. It's a pleasure! Finding the way to the tiki bar or to the pool doesn't seem to bug you, does it? That's because the change isn't being forced upon you. In that scenario, change is a discovery, and you are open to new experiences, because you have mulled over the choices and see the benefits. Indeed, under those circumstances, you court new experiences; you welcome them.

In a corporate setting, whether change is perceived positively or negatively is often a matter of how change is communicated and experienced. If the reason for and benefits of the change are carefully articulated, and the expected outcome is seen in the light of these benefits, the response to the change can be managed. So, it is essential for organizations to understand change if they are going to implement new policies, practices, or processes. I don't care whether the policies are new "no smoking" rules, new safety procedures for the forklift, or changes at the highest order of organizational structure. If the change is going to be effective, clear communication of the reasons for change, the expected outcome, and the benefits is essential. And that communication must happen before the change is implemented.

Here's a domestic example to drive this point home. When your husband or wife says, "Honey, new rule. You have to put the mayonnaise jar back in the fridge *immediately* after you use it," that can sound like a direct command from on high. But if the message is conditioned with an explanation, "Darling, I've learned that, once opened, mayonnaise will spoil and can make you very ill unless it is kept refrigerated" (the unrefrigerated contents can develop deadly bacteria)...

then you are starting to see why there has been a change in household policy. The reason for the change is clear. And the expected outcome is clear as well: Someone wants you to live long enough to pay for that trip to Hawaii. The change is an understandable win-win.

In a corporate environment, the application of human nature doesn't change much from what it is like at home. An order to change behavior, barked from on high, looks arrogant and dictatorial *if* the reason for the change and the desired outcome are not explained. Moreover, the expected outcome should show some benefit to everyone, or at least to a broad cross section of your employee base. Go back to my earlier example. If your spouse orders a change in behavior just to preserve *his or her own health* and not yours, then you have reason to be resentful. Your employees are no different. If in tough times, you order a change in pay policy and cut front line workers' salaries, while executive pay packages are maintained intact, you can easily guess what the response will be. So it is easy to understand the flare-ups that occur when organizations institute layoffs and plant closings, while paying bonuses to executives for slashing tactics that "save" the business.

However, if the leadership explains (in a authentic and believable way) the need to cut salaries across the board to prepare the company to benefit in the long run, and the leadership steps up to say that they will be the first to feel the pain, then you are allowing the effects of the change to be felt collectively. With that, you can generate some "common cause" around what you have to do.

I recall reading, in dismay, about a local North Carolina company that through a series of mismanagement steps was forced into bankruptcy. The board chose to keep the chairman and the CEO in place (huh?), and when these two execs "helped" the company emerge from Chapter 11, each was paid a "good management" bonus of more than $1 million. How could employees and former employees, investors, and suppliers trust the need for changes that those executives led?

I can think of numerous other examples to illustrate this point about clear communication and the need to articulate the reason for change, but here's a good one that the sales consultant Chip Bell tells in his presentations. He was at a small hotel one day, and he spotted a handmade sign in the lobby that said the restaurant was going to be short-staffed because of an unexpected death in the family of one of the workers. Moreover, the sign also said that some of the coworkers were also taking the day off to help the family. The sign asked for everyone's understanding. Well, if the average business traveler had come into that restaurant and been forced to endure a change (a dramatic drop in customer service) with no explanation, they would have been resistant and furious. But Chip Bell said that once the hotel guests saw that sign, they jumped in to help out! Guys were pouring coffee for each other, clearing their own tables, and adding up their own checks. See, the reason for the change was clear—a death in the family. The outcome was clear: It was time to help someone out who was in need. The collective benefits were clear: Let's help each other out for our mutual benefit. The result? People acted in the most generous fashion imaginable! They bought-in. All of them. That's the attitude toward change that you need to generate if you want it implemented with enthusiasm and success. Whether you are in a restaurant, your own kitchen, waiting at an airport gate, or in line at the store, change becomes far more tolerable when it is explained and the benefits to all, but particularly to you, are clear.

Take that example back into the corporate environment. If the reason and the outcome are clear, and the hurt (and the ensuing benefits!) are equitably distributed, you'd be amazed how people rise to the occasion. Otherwise, requests for change of nearly any magnitude are unsustainable. Indeed, without the backing of leadership, they are viewed as just half-hearted, flavor-of-the-month attempts to fix problems that just keep reemerging. That said, good corporate policies aimed at engaging employees are never wholly and perfectly formed upon conception. Before implementing a change—whether it is financial transparency, policies that encourage respect, or other policies aimed at engagement—they must be thought through, and the leadership has to be serious and forceful about the process. If you introduce a new policy and it doesn't look as though the implementation has the *sustained backing* of leadership, everyone just waits for the "sugar high" to burn off and the organization reverts back to its old ways.

If you are a leader or manager who is implementing change, be forceful. Communicate it; communicate it again. Have a plan in place for dealing with people who are passive-aggressive and recalcitrant. Those types of people will emerge, and if you don't immediately address their negative behavior, that behavior gives permission to others to act negatively; nonaction is interpreted as an indication that the leadership isn't really behind the changes being put in place.

A leader or manager must also be prepared to distribute ownership of the change throughout the entire organization. If you have a high-energy leader and that leader is looked to as a visionary, he can't be the sole bearer of the message of change, not the sole person implementing it. The ownership—and therefore the accountability—for the implementation has to be distributed to every level of the organization, to everyone in the value chain. If the organization makes a commitment to cheerleading, it can't just be the CEO who sweeps through the halls now and then to scream *rah rah*. The leadership must insist that cheerleading come from everyone, from line managers to division and regional managers, all the way up to the top of the organization's chain of command. With a consistent approach to distributing the ownership of a change in policy, the employees must see the value of the change, what's in it for them, the expected outcome, and that the organization as a whole is not just changing for change's sake. In that sense, the behavior of the leaders or managers should be exemplary, because that behavior is the model everyone looks to when deciding how to respond to change.

With that road map for implementing change in mind, let me turn to how to decide the *magnitude of change* that your organization is capable of enduring at any one time. A great many times in my career I have been asked how I implemented such "revolutionary" policy changes, especially in human resources, which is my principal practice area. I always respond that my changes were not revolutionary at all. In fact, effective change is rarely revolutionary. It is, instead, *evolutionary*. Think of examples elsewhere in the world, in any organizational structure. When a revolutionary government drops itself like a heavy-weight wrestler on a population and demands wholesale and immediate change, there is usually vast upheaval and resistance, even if everyone agrees with the change. However, if a government puts changes in place through an incremental and evolutionary process, where one step builds on another, then the change can be more readily absorbed. That kind of evolutionary change is more lasting and more sustainable because the new policies do not demand immediate acculturation and harsh adjustment, no matter what the benefits. Instead, effective change works within the existing culture to change it.

A noted expert on the topic of change, John Kotter, produced a seminal article, called "Leading Change," which was published in the *Harvard Business Review*. In that article, he focused on why employees resist change. His thesis—which will sound familiar to you by now—is that change has to be led by the executives in charge, by the CEO and the executive team. Further, the way to make change effective in an organization is for employees to be engaged by it. But for the engagement to happen, the organization has to create a "triple win" that occurs as a result of that change—that is, the change must be genuinely good for the organization, the change must benefit the employees, and the change must create or build some value for the clients, customers, and the stockholders. Without that kind of integration, the change won't be enduring, according to Kotter, and I couldn't agree more.

Let's take another approach to understanding this. The famous and notorious political philosopher Niccolo Machiavelli stated that there was nothing harder than change and leadership in a new order. (For a minute or two, please put aside your impression of Machiavelli as a cynic and advocate for supreme control and manipulation, because he did say some insightful things about change.)

Here is what he had to say:

> And let it be noted that there is no more delicate matter to take in hand, nor more dangerous to conduct, nor more doubtful in its success, than to set up (to be) as a leader in the introduction of changes. For he who innovates will have for his enemies all those who are well off under the existing order of things, and only the lukewarm supporters in those who might be better off under the new. This lukewarm temper arises partly from the fear of adversaries who have the laws on their side and partly from the incredulity of mankind, who will never admit the merit of anything new, until they have seen it proved by the event. (*The Prince*, Oxford World's Classics, Oxford University Press)

At the risk of upsetting a few of my history professors, I want to explode one myth here. As I suggested in the opening section of this rule, I don't believe people naturally resist change. Note that Machiavelli seems to be referring to change that is implemented forcefully without explanation, or with Draconian intent. As I alluded to earlier, I think people resist *being changed*. They resist someone dictating change without explanation, without generating buy-in. When people are asked to embrace change and the change is strange to them, *then* you will have a "Machiavellian response," so to speak. People tenaciously cling to the present they know rather than the future they don't know, no matter what the promise of that future. So, at the risk of sounding repetitive, make clear what the change is, articulate why it is necessary—what it's about, and then develop clear milestones and metrics of success, so the leaders can cheerlead the progress.

Two pieces of advice as you engage this process, especially when you are setting milestones and metrics for success: First, work in small increments. If you want a 15 percent change in one aspect of your business, don't push for all 15 percent in the first year, or the first six months. You may achieve that, but you may just as quickly fall backward later, because change of that magnitude is nearly impossible to sustain. So, try to move the needle five percent and then another five percent and then another five percent.

Second, don't assume that everyone understands at the granular level exactly what you are doing and why. Others may not be as competent or as skilled at reading minds and hearts as you are. When someone tells you to "implement a change in X policy," that phrase has implications to a seasoned manager that it does not have to a line worker or a new manager. The word "implement" can collectively refer to a great deal of action and protocols for you that the summary single word "implement" may not convey to someone else. Think of it this way. If you were taking a golf lesson from Tiger Woods, he might say something as simple as, "Okay, now take your backswing...." The phrase "take your backswing" means something entirely different to Tiger Woods than it does to mere mortals like you and me. His knowledge of the "backswing" is an intimate one and based on years of learning, experience, and acquired skill. Woods act of taking a backswing involves a great deal of all of the above, along with natural talent that he can't assume others naturally possess. So, explain the "what and why" of what you expect people to do in great detail. Break down your steps into increments to get the best implementation of change, much as Tiger Woods might say, "Okay, wait! Let's back up and look at this backswing as a series of smaller steps—take away, shoulder turn, hip rotation, wrist cock...."

Courtney Harrison joined the United States Olympic Committee in early 2006, after being recruited there by Peter Ueberroth to serve in the top human resources role. She was soon tapped to also be chief of member and events services as the 2008 Olympics approached. Harrison had a corporate leadership development background with American Express and GlaxoSmithKline, which made her the ideal person to bring leadership development to Ueberroth's grand plan to revive the enthusiasm for and reputation of the U.S. Olympic movement.

In 2006, with the Beijing Olympics looming large and right around the corner, The United States Olympic Committee needed to align and excite all employees—from executives to the front line food service workers—about a two year strategic plan. Previously, the organization had endured four CEOs in five years, and a number of aborted strategic plans, so the level of cynicism and distrust was running high. To counteract these well deserved emotions, the new CEO and the chief of HR made a decision to create a strategic plan designed by the *entire* organization. Understanding that the momentum of change is made or broken based on the employee engagement level, they knew they had to do things in a radically different way. It was not too far in the past that the previous senior leadership had attempted to include employees early on in the process, but the problem was that when the ultimate product was released, staffers could not recognize any of their own work. They felt disconnected, which rekindled the cycle of distrust and wasted energy.

The strategic planning process included leaders and staffers from different levels throughout the organization, which was nothing particularly new. But rather than limiting their involvement to kicking off the process with a grand flourish of speeches or memorandums, the CEO and the whole Senior Leadership Team participated and actively performed every single exercise as peers, not as hierarchical leaders. This openness gave license to the other employees in the room to surface ideas and offer constructive criticism that they had long wanted to offer. All it took was a couple brave souls to stand up and speak the truth without fear of challenge from above or reprisal. One could physically see and feel the energy in the room completely change. From that point on, the ideas started flowing like a river.

The planning initiative was then moved downward through the organization to allow the employees to experience the strategic plan and begin adding their ideas and solutions to the organization's biggest challenges. Rather than email out the new plan, or torture employees by making them sit in a dark room for two hours watching

PowerPoint slides about the plan, the USOC divided its hundreds of employees into smaller teams so they could offer ideas about each specific high level aspect of the strategic plan.

For instance, one critical area for the future of the Olympic Movement was to increase "relevancy" in the 18–34 year-old market. Each team was given material that focused on "young adults," and how companies and institutions marketed to them. The employee teams offered their ideas based on their own knowledge and experiences, supplemented by the material provided. In the end, the management and staff of the USOC had learned about each aspect of the plan and they'd had a chance to contribute to it. Not only had they learned about the plan first hand but they were excited, and more importantly took ownership, and became engaged in wanting to be a part of a successful outcome.

What started out as a huge change and a management challenge, had turned into a positive process that provided momentum for an organization that desperately needed it to be successful in Beijing and beyond. In a three month period, senior leadership demonstrated that by truly trusting the process of engaging their employees in the challenges of their business, they could change the momentum and commitment of an entire organization.

Was it a successful implementation of change? If you attended or watched the 2008 Summer Olympic Games, you already know the answer. They were a great success for America, as our country and the world were captivated by the performance and behavior of our athletes and their mentors, famous or obscure, professional or amateur, and wealthy or middle class. Because I knew the background of the changes I saw played out on TV and heard about from the media, I believe that the fundamental change in the way the USOC built its strategic plan for the Beijing Games was a major contributor to America's success, The Duke of Wellington is quoted as saying that "the Battle of Waterloo was won on the playing fields of Eton." He meant that success comes not only from heroic action, but also from thoughtful and enthusiastic preparation and planning.

Let's close out this rule with a look at the *J Curve*, and how to use it to ensure that change is embraced, even by those resistant to it. The J Curve is a concept advanced by Dr. Jerry Jellison, a professor at the University of Southern California, and he claims (rightly so, in my humble opinion) that the usual methods of communication are not enough to deal with resistance to change, if the resistance is from people who are emotionally hanging onto their present situation. Jellison says that people's emotional response to change can be plotted on a curve that we can visualize as the letter "J," with the top of the "J" as the launching point of change, and the "hook" of the "J," as the beginning of the imbedding of the change—that is, the new norm. The J Curve exists in five stages, from resistance through acceptance. The first stage is the starting point, the work-a-day world, which we can visualize as a plateau. As change is introduced, questioned, and looked at suspiciously, there is the second stage: the cliff. I like to call this "the panic-filled bungee-jump moment." People are in free fall with the change, with all the associated gut wrenching, and productivity drops right along with them. Stage three is when the bungee cord tightens and people bottom out, accept the change as inevitable, and start to believe that maybe they'll live through the experience. In stage four, performance and productivity return to old levels and then improve, as change takes hold and a new confidence pervades the organization's culture. With stage five, your organization's productivity rises far higher than when you started to implement that change. Of course, all this assumes the various elements I introduced earlier in this rule: communication, buy-in, distributed ownership, a great plan, and the transparently clear triple win. Are you ready to step up and embrace change? Your most aggressive competitor is, so why not try it.

16

Cultivate Organizational Ethics; Demand and Reward Ethical Behavior

In the first rule, "Understand Why Employees Come and Why They Stay," I wrote about the reasons people work. One key reason is that they want to make their "contribution to the world" at a place that is worthy of that effort and deserving of the fruits of the result. Well, one of the pillars of being a "worthy" company is to have integrity, and to possess integrity a company must behave and operate ethically. Indeed, the ethical ways of behaving and doing business must begin with the values of the company and extend through all its policies, practices, and people.

If you want engaged employees, really engaged employees who are aligned with your organizational goals, you can't run your organization on the "wink" basis. You can't allow an account manager to pad expense reports, only to have those expenses approved by a "winking" manager and a permissive accounting clerk. You can't have a rule for per diem travel expenses yet tolerate a regional sales director who breaks those rules, as he winks to a trainee that he'll "pick up" the dinner and drinks bill, so that the newbie can pocket a few bucks. And you can't have a policy where the travel coordinator cannot accept any gift worth more than $10 or any lunch of a greater value than $25, while the director of purchasing is on a two-day vendor "outing" at Pebble Beach. If a mailroom clerk is disciplined for taking a few packing boxes home to help his daughter move into her new apartment, why is it that a vice president's business trip that includes a one-day rest stop in Las Vegas is ignored. The senior leadership can't wink their way through a meeting, a meal, or a trip to a fancy bar, knowing that they are violating the organization's rules on entertainment allowances. In short, the "game" of ethics and integrity must be played on a level field, or the game gets out of control for a company.

Organizations lose on two planes when questionable business ethics and uneven enforcement of ethics standards are in play. First, when the word gets out that bending the rules is the way of things, rules get bent. Then the boundaries of what is acceptable (what can be gotten away with) are tested. Then the new "ethics" are communicated through unofficial channels, and then there are two sets of standardized ethics—how we say we behave, and how we behave.

Second, when employees see small and somewhat "harmless" violations being actively prosecuted and disciplined, while larger violations are ignored, they take stock and see the tight enforcement is for the little guy with the less-influential job. They also see that the view on ethics is different for the powerful and influential "corner office" types, with summer homes and country clubs memberships (company subsidized) and stock portfolios. Respect for, and trust in, the leadership, the company, and what it stands for quickly wanes. And a new ethic is planted: "Take care of myself; get all I can; and watch my back." A cynical, selfish, and vigilant employee cannot be engaged. She is far too busy.

What are the consequences if behavior isn't ethical? You don't just start down a slippery slope, you *tumble* down the slope and crash in a heap at the bottom. The bond of trust between the organization and the employee precipitously falls apart, and it affects your competitive edge.

Do you want an example that you might be able to relate to? Ever cheat on your taxes? Even a little? A teeny itzy bit? If you have ever done that, I'll bet you feel a sense of permission to act that way, because you know other people are doing it. No one wants to be played the fool. So, if you know others might be taking some additional allowances on their itemized 1040s, why shouldn't you? When you do this, you are, in a sense, "winking" to everyone who is filing on April 15.

You know that you are part of a larger club of winkers. Oddly, it may seem that no one is really cheating, if everyone is taking the extra allowances, right?

Well, what if you knew there was 100 percent compliance on tax filings by every U.S. citizen? And what if all corporations paid a fair tax, as judged by wide consensus? I bet few people would take an extra allowance or two on their tax forms, no matter what the level of enforcement and auditing. Moreover, I bet that most of the extra allowances taken on itemized tax forms don't really amount to that much on the bottom line. Without gross errors in reporting, it's hard to "move the needle" when trying to reduce your tax bill. In fact, I suspect that people allow themselves this behavior (which I bet is uncharacteristic within the overall scale of their individual lives) because they don't feel *everyone else* is being honest. So, ironically, cheating becomes a way to make things seem fair.

That same interpersonal dynamic is no different in an office setting. If people see unethical behavior—an exaggerated expense report, a fudged time card, a shopping bag full of pilfered office supplies—all done with a wink, many employees take this as permission to do the same. Oh, you say, it's only a roll of tape, a box of pens, and a few dollars either way. But that type of behavior has a tendency to snowball in ways that not only compromise the organization's reputation among customers and vendors, but it "blackens the soul" of the organization in the view of the employees. Employees invariably think less of a company that tolerates this kind of behavior. They might even think less of the organization if it is bumbling along unaware of (and thereby unconcerned about) such workplace behavior. But what's most damaging about this scenario is that there is a short distance between small-scale unethical behavior and large-scale violations. Would you really expect an organization that is blind to an expense report violation to clamp down on the violation of an antifraternization policy? Or minor misappropriation of funds? Or "patty cake" relationships with a vendor? Or worse, the unethical treatment of a customer via price fixing or gouging? If this kind of behavior goes unchecked in an organizational culture of disregard for ethics, it should come as no surprise to you that a highly confidential "top 100" customer profile list finds its way outside the approved distribution, or the business strategy for a new product introduction lands in the inbox of a competitor, or there is flagrant disregard of a nondisclosure agreement (NDA), putting you in legal jeopardy.

Beyond the competitive disadvantage presented by this kind of behavior, far worse deeper damage can be done to your organization at the *cultural* level, at the *visceral* level, with ethical lapses of any magnitude: Jaded employees aren't proud to go to work for you nor are they proud to tell others about their workplace. This means that potential employees, potential customers, and potential vendors don't hear good things about your organization, if they hear anything at all. A vortex is created in which the organization's brand races to the bottom, losing talented employees, and becomes unable to hire talented replacements, retain customers, and maintain valuable and fruitful vendor and contractor relationships. After all, it's only human nature not to speak with pride about shameful behavior, and unethical behavior is shameful behavior. It's only human nature to whisper to someone at a barbeque or a church gathering that such-and-such company has been known to play fast and loose with facts, figures, and behavior.

What's worse, when an organization spins downward due to unethical behavior, it's an enormous challenge to recover. By historical analogy, look at the culture of bribery that rules some third-world countries. Once an official at any station or of any status within the official hierarchy is seen taking a bribe, and that act goes unpunished, then others in the system feel as though it is perfectly okay to accept bribes. They feel like fools if they don't. Whether the unethical behavior originates at the top or the bottom of the official hierarchy, it pervades the entire hierarchy with great speed. Just so you can see how hard it is to root out, I want you to name just one country where the bribery problem has been defeated after it has entrenched itself. Can you name one? I can't.

In fact, organizations the world over are staffed by people who share a global commonality: *human nature*. And a permissive culture of unethical behavior—whether exhibited by someone taking home a cartridge of ink toner or accepting a multimillion dollar bribe to open a port to oil exports—yields the same damaging result.

With the negative effects of an unethical culture abundantly clear, note that *ethical* behavior can have an equally dramatic *positive* effect on an organization. In fact, organizations that stand up, take an ethical stand, and practice what they preach allow the employees to take that message into the public sphere, to church, to school, to their social relationships. They become ambassadors who carry a message of pride and honor into a wider community that invariably includes potential new hires, contractors, vendors, *and* new customers. Imagine your own response to a story your neighbor or golf buddy might relate about a company that summarily fired a senior executive for submitting a false expense report. Or of the wealthy CEO who adheres to the same per-diem travel and entertainment allowance as the front line manager. It sets a tone, and that tone rings as clear as a church bell among the ranks. In that sense, ethical behavior can build *esprit de corps* to great heights. Indeed, even with all this high-flung talk about how organizations should behave, it ultimately comes down to a truism that you probably heard before you got to kindergarten: *What's good for the goose is good for the gander*. Oh, and one other thing: There is no honor among thieves.

Let's take this up another level. There are two types of ethics: internal and external. Internal ethics apply to such matters as respect to one another, fair treatment in workplace dealings, limited political behavior, limited agendas that aren't in service of the company's goals, and zero-tolerance for cheating. External ethics apply to such matters as treating customers, clients, and vendors fairly; paying people on time; creating a level playing field for everyone who is doing business with you; and creating win-win scenarios for your customers and vendors.

A few years ago, Minitab, a company discussed earlier in this book, changed its pricing structure to include a single fee for companies that would purchase and install large numbers of Minitab's products for multiyear periods. These "enterprise" licenses were offered at discounts that reflected the confidence the buyers showed in Minitab and its products and were also a reflection of the solid relationships between vendor and customer.

As this purchasing option was being rolled up, the sales force informed the management team of the fact that a substantial group of loyal customers had expanded their use of the company's software to a point that, although they were operating under old and still binding contractual agreements, any renewal would make them eligible for the newly instituted discounts. What did Minitab do? They immediately contacted those customers and advised them of a reduction in license fees—with a rollback to the date of the commencement of the discounted pricing. Now, that is ethical Customer Relationship Management!

With that in mind, let's look further at the implications of ethical behavior on cost avoidance and workplace culture. An ethical workplace is a great tool for recruiting prospective employees—as I pointed out earlier—and it is also a great tool for the acculturation of new employees. If a front line manager is relating the travel policy or work-from-home policies to a new recruit, and the manager relates honestly that a very high percentage of people who work for the organization adhere to these rules, I confidently predict that the new recruit will 1) find the ethical compliance of the other employees admirable, 2) recognize that the company is practicing what it preaches, 3) relate this story to others outside the company, and 4) let this ethical culture inform his actions in other areas of corporate practice. That spirit alone can lead to a dramatic competitive advantage, because engaged employees of an ethical organization draw other ethical employees, and that workforce draws customers and prospects who want to work with an organization whose ethics are uncompromised.

Let me take another approach to this topic, because I suspect that one or two readers are saying, "Come on, no company is that pure. When people cut corners now and then, exaggerate an expense, or take some extra time off without the boss's knowledge, that's just the way of the world. After all, everyone does it!"

But is it? Is it the way of the world?

A great deal of this book has been focused on getting organizations to be run as **meritocracies** (where people advance on the basis of their contribution and its value), and not as systems where people or ideas are promoted for reasons other than their inherent value. So, let me ask you, if it's the "way of the world" to cheat now and then, why has competiveness, excellence, profitability, and overall company value consistently risen over time as ethical practices have been codified and modeled by like-minded companies? Each year, as the list of the most-corrupt countries is published, why are the countries at the bottom of the barrel invariably the ones rated as the worse places to do business, the least fruitful places to start businesses, and the most poverty-stricken? It's because the merit of an idea does not advance its cause. But isn't it only a matter of degrees between a corrupt nation and an organization corrupted (however incrementally) by unethical behavior? Look at the top companies in the world, the most-admired companies in the world, and I assure you that you see a direct correlation between their ethical behavior and their success. What's more, you see the behavior modeled from the top, by the leadership, without exception.

If you want a recent example, look no further than the banking crisis of 2008. Companies that had strict ethical lending practices, such as Goldman Sachs and JP Morgan Chase, emerged with far less damage to their overall company value than the companies that greedily played fast and loose with the rules, where employees winked at each other when they should have spoken up and taken corrective action. Before the banking crisis, take a look at Enron, whose unethical, predatory practices and serial deceptions drained billions of dollars of value from a company that was at one time on top of the world.

If organizations do the right thing, behave the right way, play fair, are not cannibals, and are not predatory, they are actually moving contrary to the historical "might makes right" tradition. Though "might makes right" may work in the short term, or as long as you have "the might," eventually the merit of good ideas wins out and "*right* makes might" becomes the prevailing catchphrase. In today's lightning-fast global economy, where there is increased transparency, and data is freely transferred in universal digital languages, the "cycle time" to expose a bully or to expose unethical behavior and corruption is much faster, and the unethical company reaps the consequences far sooner than they would have in 1940 or 1840 or 1740.

That said, employee engagement at the highest level needs to be based on ethical behavior, yet most companies don't seem to find it all that interesting to have the high ethical standing as a compelling strategy for their operations. A recent Ethics Research Center newsletter circulated the results of a 2008 survey that polled human resources executives. The survey found that 23 percent of those surveyed said that their organization had a comprehensive ethical compliance program in place. A full 7 percent of those surveyed said that their organization doesn't pay any attention to ethics. If those numbers are right, a full 77 percent (more than three-quarters of all companies!) have *no* policies or ethics programs. The same survey found that fewer than half the people surveyed said that ethical conduct is part of a managers' or executives' performance appraisal. And 57 percent said that ethics plays *no part* in the front line employee's performance reviews.

If this is the situation, then organizations don't put much value on ethics, or they don't behave ethically. Can these companies really expect to gain a competitive advantage with aligned employees? The de facto message being communicated to these employees is that unethical behavior and activity is tolerated at their place of work, or at least not actively regulated. So, what can you expect employees to say to that—that they are proud to work there? Do you expect that they speak highly of the company in all their social and professional

interactions? Or course not! Instead they say, "Why should I value ethical principles if no one else is acting in accordance with those principles, and especially when the company won't even say what they are!?"

To retain good people who are ethical, you have to behave ethically. And the way to attract ethical people is by having a "brand," a reputation as an employer for ethical behavior. For obvious reasons, that
behavior doesn't just spontaneously appear in company policy, even
though I believe that the capacity for ethical behavior is inherent in us
all. So, the ethical policies and rules need to be written down someplace public and communicated in a regular, disciplined, and standardized manner. Then those policies should be supported across the
board, and a method should be created to allow employees to report
violations without fear of retaliation, from inside or out. You can't have
a policy to encourage whistle blowing and then allow the whistle
blower to be ostracized and iced out. Indeed, that is the kind of person
who should be publicly rewarded, in much the same way you should
reward stellar examples of ongoing compliance with your ethics policy.

Next, new employees should undergo an orientation and socialization process to introduce them to the ethical policies. Moreover,
there should be an FAQ resource for "gray areas" where a new or
legacy employee might wonder what the best course is to take on
certain matters. That FAQ can be online, or it can be a person who
is designated to answer such questions.

To underscore all these actions, ethical behavior must be part of a
rewards and punishment system, as I have alluded throughout this
rule. A standard should be set and communicated, and all employees,
without exception, should be measured with the same yardstick
against that standard. You can't fire the mail clerk for a violation that
is tolerated by someone more powerful. Behavior like that would
rightly be perceived as hypocritical, and you would immediately lose
faith and face with the employees. Indeed, people's intolerance for
hypocrisy is, I think, as universal and pervasive as people's inherent
capacity for ethical behavior, *if* they see that they are not being played

the fool and that ethical behavior is appropriately rewarded and unethical behavior accordingly punished.

What I have suggested in this rule is consistent with the other practices recommended in other places in the book. Policies must be established with good reason and the best intentions. The policies must be transparent and applicable to all. The policies must be communicated consistently and publicly. Violations of policies must be recognized and appropriately dealt with, no matter how powerful the violator nor how powerless the victim. With transparency, communication, consistency, and enforcement, you win not only the respect *and participation* of your employees, but you win the respect and participation of your customers, vendors, contractors, and extended communities. You also win a remarkable level of competitive advantage, and that competitive advantage is not just a "sugar high" that you achieved with an underhanded deal, but an *enduring advantage* gained through deliberate actions that can be modeled and replicated at any scale.

Let me close with an exemplary story about how ethical behavior and great leadership can contribute to making a great company. KeySpan Energy is a company formed by the merger of Brooklyn Union Gas and Long Island Lighting Company (a.k.a. LILCO). It's a big operation, with a great deal riding on its daily performance, and there isn't any room for inappropriate behavior. A while ago, the CEO there, a fellow by the name of Robert Catell, told a story at a New York gathering of "thought leaders" about a unique practice he put into place some years before. He asked his managers to regularly inform him of employees who were doing great work. Then he made it a point to call these employees privately, one by one, to personally thank them for their efforts and to let them know how essential their work was for the company's overall success. One woman he called was an office administrator, and she was flabbergasted to get a call from the chief executive officer. Not fully aware of the degree to which she was surprised and impressed by the call, Catell carried on with his genuine praise of her work. He ended the call without thinking much more of it.

A few years later, it was this very woman who exposed a senior executive for malfeasance. After all was said and done, the executive was disciplined and fired. But Catell was curious as to why this woman, of all people, had come forth. So he called her again. He asked her why a woman like herself, without much stature or status in the company, would come forth. After all, to speak candidly, she was a small fish is a very large pond. Yet she did the right thing, without fear of being ostracized or even dismissed for speaking truth to power. She told Catell that she remembered when he had called that first time; she said that she found it remarkable that a CEO would care so much about the people within the company that he would call an individual employee to thank her for her work and her contribution. She told him that she just knew that a company and a CEO who cared enough to thank her personally (years ago!) would never let any unfairness befall her for doing the right thing now. And you know what? She was right.

As Yvette Rauff, who is second in command at Minitab, tells her employees, "In any situation, if you can see the line that crosses over from ethical to questionable behavior, you are already too close!"

Compliance is what you do when someone else is keeping score; ethics is displayed when you are the scorekeeper.

17

The Last and Overarching Rule: Tell the Truth! (and a Few Action Items to Grow On)

In the movie *A Few Good Men*, there is a memorable scene where Tom Cruise, as defense counsel, confronts witness Jack Nicholson, a veteran marine colonel. After they exchange a few barbs, Nicholson baits Cruise, "What do you want!?"

Cruise responds, "I want the truth!"

Nicholson's comeback is, "You want the truth? You can't handle the truth!"

I think of this scene fairly often and smile to myself when I see executives and managers "dumbing down" the messages they give to employees. Truths are "spun" into "company speak" so that what is really going on with a sticky situation is clouded over beyond recognition. Fact is, many people in positions of power and influence just don't understand that you can't lie—even little lies, white lies—to the people on whom you depend for success and prosperity. The result is that those people feel as though you don't think they count. Those people feel as though you think they are stupid, unworthy, and not to be trusted.

> "Truth is like the sun. You can block it out for a time, but it ain't goin' away."
>
> —*Elvis Presley*

Worse, they will hate you for it. Yes, I said *hate*.

But I don't mean the kind of explosive hate that we see depicted in films or on TV. I mean the gnawing hate that surfaces in far-less-obvious ways. "You think I'm stupid? Well, I'm smart enough to fool you!" "You don't trust me to know? I'll show you how much I know!" "What I think doesn't count? Oh yeah, well, count this!" Those phrases sum up the active dislike of the ownership, management, and organization that can arise when employees feel compelled to respond with hatred, and that can disrupt the organization's present and corrupt its future.

> **"A half truth is a whole lie."**
>
> —*Yiddish Proverb*

Whenever the opportunity arises, I ask leaders why they couch the truth in nonsense and company speak. The answer is generally the same. Leaders are afraid that the whole truth cannot be "handled well" by the employees. When I press for what "handled well" means, the responses are fascinating and even amusing. The leaders fear leaks of proprietary data, fear of creating fear or anger, fear of defection from the ranks, fear of emotional and contagious negative responses—the list goes on. My amusement comes from the apparent lack of "people knowledge" these leaders have accumulated over their years in business. They are unable to understand that the people they are protecting from the truth are the same people who deal with divorce, family tragedy, financial setbacks, serious illnesses, child rearing, college tuition, and elder care issues. These leaders fail to understanding that their employees deal with truths far more gut-wrenching and emotional than nearly anything an honest company communication will offer. In fact, they often deal with those stresses and setbacks on a daily basis.

> **"In a time of universal deceit, telling the truth becomes a revolutionary act."**
>
> —*George Orwell*

> **"When in doubt, tell the truth."**
>
> —*Mark Twain*

But the worst is that most people have active and highly sensitive "BS monitors." They easily see through the half-truths. When truth goes missing and the truth is required to make sense of things, people tend to scan the world around them and find the truth. In an effort to determine what's really going on, they gather bits and pieces of their own evidence. Then they come up with the "truth" and adjust behavior and attitude based on *their truth*. The saddest part to this is that the "new" truth is the perception that becomes reality, and nothing management says can dispel it. So, the entire activity of "truth finding" damages trust and fosters passive-aggressive behaviors.

A veteran Minitab nonmanagement employee told me a story about the effects of truthfulness that speaks loudly about its value in building and sustaining a great company. Back in the early 1990s Minitab was having some tough times. Sales were slack; money was tight. There was even the remote possibility that the company might not survive. The employees knew that there was trouble and began to fear the possibility of layoffs.

> "Truth fears no questions."
> —*Unknown*

Ken Falkenbach, Minitab's first COO, gathered all the employees together and told them, in detail, the nature of the crisis—he laid it all bare before them. It was painful; it was the unvarnished truth. Then he declared that, in spite of the situation, Minitab would do whatever it would take to avoid cutting staff. He expressed confidence that, if they all took a temporary pay cut to stem the tide and came up with a few additional cost-cutting measures, they would be okay.

> "The truth needs so little rehearsal."
> —*Barbara Kingsolver*

The employees took Ken's candor and commitment as a rallying cry. A number of suggestions were offered, but the most memorable

> "Truth exists; only falsehood has to be invented."
> —*Georges Braque*

> "Three things cannot be long hidden: the sun, the moon, and the truth."
>
> *—Buddha*

among them was to interrupt the use of many outside services and to have employees take on and share those previously outsourced tasks. For a period of months, employee volunteers cleaned offices, hauled trash, refilled toilet tissue dispensers, and even swabbed commodes to support their company.

Today Minitab employees remember those difficult days with fondness, and they describe that period of time to new hires as a coalescing experience, and a first indication of what the company could and would become.

Last Rules

So now, let's look at some overarching rules that can be followed to move an organization to become an engaged workplace. In short, there are just a few things that leaders and executives need to do to build a work environment that nurtures employee commitment to the mission and purposes of the company:

- Leaders must make sure all employees know what is expected of them and what things they can expect from the company and its leadership.
- Leaders must oversee a culture that treats people with respect and care.
- Leaders must provide resources and be a resource themselves.
- Leaders must own the responsibility for downward communication that is regular and clear, and they must require the same of mid- and lower-level managers.

  Leaders must behave in a way that builds trust, confidence, understanding, and a visceral relationship between employees and company, and leaders must visibly model that behavior and demand it from their subordinates.

- Finally, leaders must operate the company and pursue success in a transparent fashion.

You may have seen *The Bucket List*, a popular 2008 movie starring Jack Nicholson and Morgan Freeman. Two characters list the things they want to do before they die. Well, I have my own list to show you, but it's not a "bucket list" of things to do before you die. It's a list of the things you should do if you (as an organization) intend to thrive and live! These items aren't the last things you should be doing but the first things you should undertake. Like now.

Is your organization ready to build a way of behaving and conducting business that improves the likelihood of attracting and keeping people? And do you want those people to be loyal, engaged, productive, and aligned with the organization's goals? I've laid out a list of to-do's for you. To keep the list manageable (and the book small enough to carry in one hand), I have limited the to-do's to one or two for each of the sixteen previous rules.

If you manage to adopt six or more of the rules as leadership guides, and you are able to implement six or more of the suggested items from the list, I can promise you a wholly different and improved work environment, as well as a far more engaged and productive workforce. So, get about changing your company!

Rule #1—Why They Come and Why They Stay

1. Take a new approach to employee orientation. As a standard aspect of orientation, create a conversation with all new employees about what they can expect from the company, its management, and other employees. Make sure that each new hire hears from someone (of status and authority) all that is expected of employees with regard to work ethic, productivity, and behavior.

2. Executives should participate in orienting new hires. Require that at least one senior management person communicates an official welcome to all new hires, and that the senior management expresses confidence that the new hire will have a great opportunity and be a valuable contributor to company success.

Rule #2—Play "Win-Win"

3. Make a concerted effort to build an internal communications system that is biased toward clear explanations of decisions; communicate how the execution of plans benefits the customer, the company, and the individual.

4. Enforce a ban on office politics. Let those in power positions know that political maneuvering and manipulation of data, situations, or people will be treated with swift and visible discipline. Let the employees know that they are working in an environment where they don't have to watch their back, or worse, CYA.

Rule #3—Cultivate Leadership

5. Find your leaders and train them in the skills of leadership. A plethora of "leadership" development experiences are available for purchase. Yet have you noticed that the quality of leadership in our organizations is not improving—regardless of the dollars spent? Maybe the wrong people are being exposed to the opportunity.

6. Executives should look for leadership qualities in their people, and begin to concentrate time and money on those who have a natural talent for and interest in leadership. You can train a person to be a manager, but you can only develop inherent leadership qualities already in the possession of individuals.

Rule #4—Provide Resources

7. You want your staff to be successful, and it's up to them to choose the path to that success. That said, conveying resources and control to the employee indicates how you feel about them, either positive or negative. So, hand over control of resources to someone who is inextricably linked to the success (or failure) of the project. That will motivate them to take ownership of the project and to invest pride and extra effort in doing it well.

8. To convey the expectations that accompany resources, the manager should express that he sees something in an employee or subordinate; the manager should verbalize that he recognizes the employee's or subordinate's talents and skills; that the employee's or subordinate's potential is clear, that you want to see it actualized, and here are the tools to make it happen.

Rule #5—Demand Contribution; Be Worthy of Receiving It

9. *Don't demand effort; demand contribution.* And the only way to effectively demand contribution is to show employees where their contribution adds to the big picture, where an employee's contribution adds to the organization's overall goals.

10. A carefully nurtured culture is only part of the battle to draw an employee's best possible contribution. The culture has to be regularly communicated, so the employee recognizes what part she plays in the company's progress and the customer experience. The employee must be told what a contribution means and what it looks like, and she must be told that contribution is what is expected, what counts, and what will be counted.

Rule #6—Applaud Effort; Reward Contribution

11. It's toxic to reward effort. If you start to reward effort, the people really making contributions will see their efforts as denigrated. So, don't reward the churners, at the same level that you are rewarding the people who are propelling the organization forward. The contributors will see that rewards are tied to the wrong metrics and that the company is indeed rewarding motion not results.

12. Punishing people isn't a good use of time and energy. It's not a sincere effort to motivate a deadbeat employee, and it ends up being focused on revenge. If someone isn't capable of focusing on outcomes, there's little you can do with that person anyway, as he is unmanageable. There's little that can motivate him...except the powerful force of withholding recognition and rewards.

Rule #7—Become a Cheerleader

13. It's not childish to cheerlead, because you have to let the employees know that they're doing a good job. You'd be surprised how much employees crave a little encouragement, and how quickly that encouragement translates to high levels of commitment.

14. It's wrong to think that all people invariably want is more money. Pay and benefits are just substitutes for warmth, caring, and recognition of worth. Don't set up your organization so that the only way you can express your appreciation for an employee's value is with money, you'll find it's just not enough; it's *never* enough.

Rule #8—Build on Respect

15. By not giving and demanding respect in the workplace, organizations become politicized, and you are destined for decline when ideas and initiatives are not judged on their merits but on the personal allegiances of people within the organization.

16. Recognize that the workplace has replaced the family social circle. It's a *club* that meets every day, and workmates engage with their extended "family" at work very much as they did with a blood-related family decades ago. At work, we seek advice, we commiserate, we support each other, we argue...and we trust each other.

Rule #9—Cultivate Trust

17. Trust must flow from leaders and managers to employees, but it also must flow back from employees, and employees have to trust that the leadership cares about them, not only as a means to an end, but as *people*. So, you must demonstrate that you care about what your people care about.

18. Leaders have to communicate the truth while being clear about what they expect from people. Organizations should have transparent financials, processes, and decision-making. That's a key element for fostering teamwork, trust, and camaraderie.

Rule #10—Make Room for Fun

19. Pride yourself on building and nurturing a healthy and creative work environment by believing and behaving as though your people—given resources, guidance, and recognition—will amaze you with what they can accomplish.

20. Introduce fun into the workplace. Foster lightheartedness. Leaders and managers should be pleasant to be around. Remember that fun in the workplace is not mutually exclusive to productivity. Indeed, one actually *enhances* the other.

Rule #11—Seek Alignment

21. Cultivate engaged employees by building "linking opportunities" between an organization's wants, needs, and culture and the issues that drive what the employees' care about. The first steps for creating that alignment is to know your employees at a very deep level.

22. Establish an open culture where employees feel integral and essential to the organization. They must feel as though they are directly contributing to the organization's goals. When employees are aligned with the organization's values and mission, and the organization displays its respect for individuals, employees will engage more actively. Guaranteed.

Rule #12—Understand Human Capital

23. Human capital can also be understood as the wealth-generating potential that exists within the people who work for an organization, and it embraces all facets of their knowledge, skills, and intellectual properties; it encompasses the skills, experiences, *and effort* of your workforce. It is their ability (and their willingness) to "do" things on behalf of the enterprise.

24. Progressive, insightful human resources experts (and I like to put myself in that category) have had to work very hard to discourage organizations and management from looking at people as nothing more than interchangeable parts. We have made an effort to show that people are just as valuable to organizations as the buildings and the equipment that the organization owns, maintains, and invests in. In short, organizations need to see their people as investments, and each one individually unique.

Rule #13—Treat Employees as Volunteers

25. Remember that your employees are volunteers; treat them as such. The labor market will not always favor the employer. Your challenge? Get your own employees to *want* to come back to work each week, to *want* to boost your competitive advantages, to want to contribute at the highest level possible for the tasks assigned. You can meet that challenge by behaving as though you really need them to show up again tomorrow.

26. Employees are far more willing to consider other work options, *all the time*. They are willing to risk their skills and aptitudes in the marketplace, including the skills you taught them. Any hint of a "plantation mentality" on the part of management is justification for the employee to seek work elsewhere.

Rule #14—Know the Culture

27. Survey your employees and regularly ask questions about their feelings about how the company is doing. Ask if they believe they are learning, growing, and contributing, and if management is doing a good job. Ask if management is communicating well, behaving appropriately, and listening to comments, suggestions, complaints, and feedback from employees.

28. Follow up on survey responses that indicate trends and consensus with clear answers about what you heard, what will be done, what will be considered, and what is not possible. Then, take high-profile action that is focused and clearly connected to the feedback.

Rule #15—Understand Change

29. Whether change is perceived positively or negatively is often a matter of how change is communicated and experienced. The response to the change can be managed, if the reason for and benefits of the change are carefully articulated, and the expected outcome is seen in the light of these benefits.

30. If you are implementing change, be forceful. Communicate it; communicate it again. Have a plan in place for dealing with people who are passive-aggressive and recalcitrant. Those types of people will emerge, and if you don't immediately address their negative behavior, that behavior gives permission to others to act negatively; nonaction is interpreted as an indication that the leadership isn't really behind the changes being put in place.

Rule #16—Cultivate Ethics

31. The consequences of unethical behavior are that you don't just start down a slippery slope, you *tumble* down the slope and crash in a heap at the bottom. The bond of trust between the organization and the employee precipitously falls apart, and it affects your competitive edge.

32. Beyond the competitive disadvantage presented by unethical behavior, far worse deeper damage can be done to your organization, at the *cultural* level, at the *visceral* level, with ethical lapses of any magnitude: Jaded employees won't be proud to go to work for you nor will they be proud to tell others about their workplace, turning away potential employees, customers, and vendors.

INDEX